Melanie Jackson

Commissioned by Cardiff Bay Arts Trust
123 Stryd Bute
Caerdydd CF1 6AE
123 Bute Street
Cardiff CF1 6AE
T (01222) 488772
F (01222) 472439
www.cbat.co.uk

ISBN 0 907623 33 6

Published by
Matt's Gallery
42–44 Copperfield Road
London E3 4RR
T (020) 8983 1771
F (020) 8983 1435

Melanie Jackson

soil & seawater

With an essay by Ian Hunt

Matt's Gallery, London 1999

It was impossible to gaze upon this tumultuous sea of mountains without being deeply affected with their terrible majesty and awful grandeur ... It must be set down to the credit of photography that it teaches the mind to see the beauty and power of such scenes as these and renders it more susceptible of their sweet and elevating impressions. For my own part, I must say that before I commenced photography I did not see half the beauties in nature that I do now.

S Bourne 'Ten weeks with a camera in the Himalayas'
in British Journal of Photography, **15 February 1864**

Friends of mine who visit watch this light show with different eyes. They prefer the page of the landscape to the text of the neon. They seem to think it's more 'authentic'. I, on the other hand, suspect that authenticity is altogether elsewhere, that they are responding to nature's ability to mimic the sincerity of a painting, that the question of the sunset and The Strip is more a matter of one's taste in duplicity.

Dave Hickey 'A Rhinestone As Big As The Ritz'
Air Guitar, **1997**

The identification of England with the island is already, and from the start, a fiction. It is a fiction, but an unwavering one amongst English writers and other English people, that England occupies the land up to the margins of every shore. The island has seemed the perfect form in English cultural imagining, as the city was to the Greeks. Defensive, secure, compacted, even paradisal – a safe place; a safe place too from which to set out on predations and from which to launch the building of an empire.

Gillian Beer

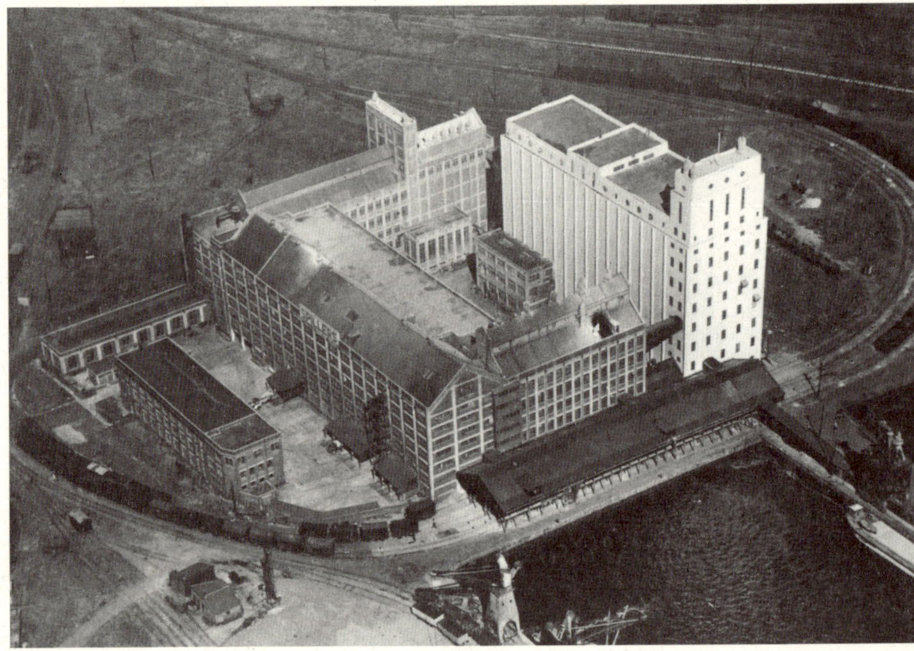

The whole dock is built on a floating base, all reclaimed land. The Mill is a 'single pour' structure, whereby concrete was poured into a 220 yard long, 180 yard high shuttering, in one long continuous flow. It is the biggest in Europe, and was the pride of its founder Leo Spillers. News stories of the time all compare it to a cathedral. When he was inspecting the growing construction he grazed his leg on some iron reinforcement and eventually lost his life to the injury when gangrene set in the wound. The factory complex is demolished now, but the Mill will stand for posterity: it has recently been protected as a Building of Merit.

The Mill stands out in the Dock. Regal. A beacon amidst stockpiles and ghost ships. The new factories down here work silently, flexi-time. No obvious shift patterns, no smoke, no sirens. Occasional ships still pass by on giddy small scale, long distance export ventures. (Grain for Saudi racehorses, dyed an indelible pink to keep it from appearing at the wrong table, a surplus harvest bound for Korea.) But it all feels like a matter of time. New industries and new industrialists are being advertised for. The manager has worked here thirty-eight years, his stories meander sixty. He pulls out a postcard of the mill from the air – the building really was used as a beacon. Copies of the card were issued to the Luftwaffe as a navigational aide, and were carried in top pockets when flying overhead on missions east.

He recalls a more recent tale, of driving into a depot in the hollow of a nearby mountain, to contribute his quota of flour to the vast underground store, on the orders of the Ministry. He describes a great white sea of sacks, mounting load by load – a mountain of flour. This sea is tidal, the sacks rotate to keep the supply fresh. Every so often, a load is removed and so much per tonne mixed back into breadflour.

I drive around Brecon, hoping to chance upon the depot, but only run into a large area marked on the map with DANGER. There is a road running through it. A sign at the entrance says, DO NOT TOUCH ANYTHING. IT MAY EXPLODE AND KILL YOU. I don't. I film from the window. The perimeter runs beyond the horizon all around. There is no obvious sign of my flour mountain.

A letter informs me that these food supplies are no longer necessary and that the last 'buffer depot' was closed in 1995. The sites are not on record. No archive. No addresses. The Manager supposes the depot has been sold on. As if to compensate he tells more mountain tales. The first was full of treasure. Art Treasure. He talks of great paintings buried deep in the Snowdonian Mountains. The second is Epynt, the range I drove through. He tells me of its ghost villages. Later I find a pamphlet named *Epynt Without People*.

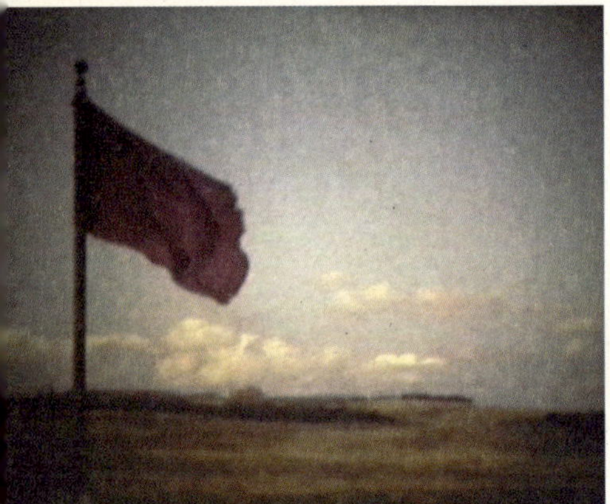
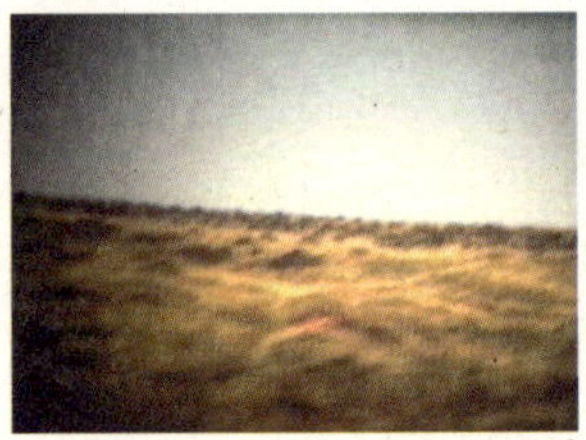
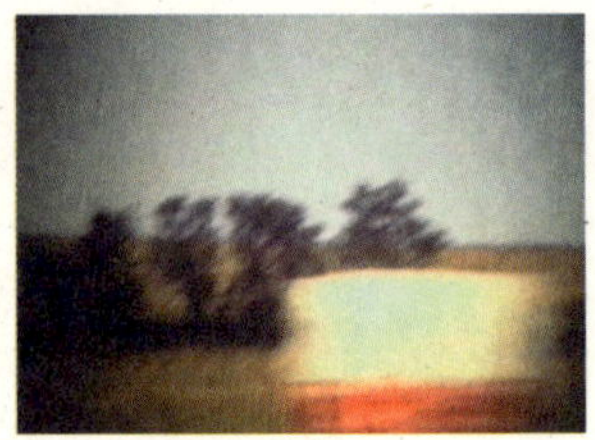
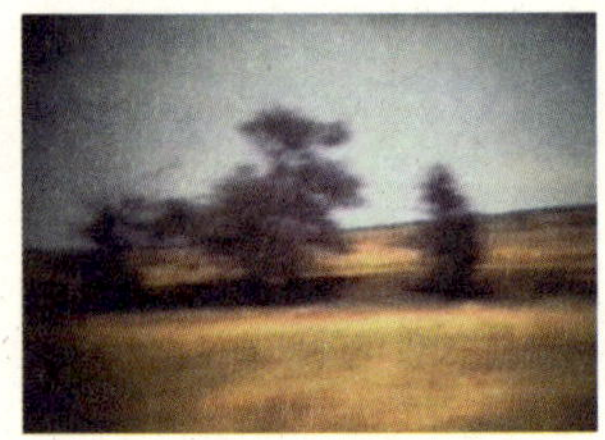
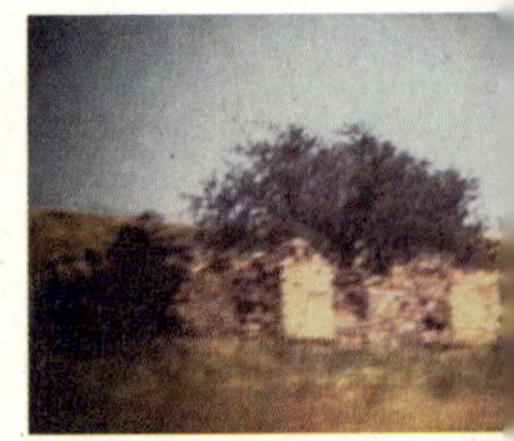

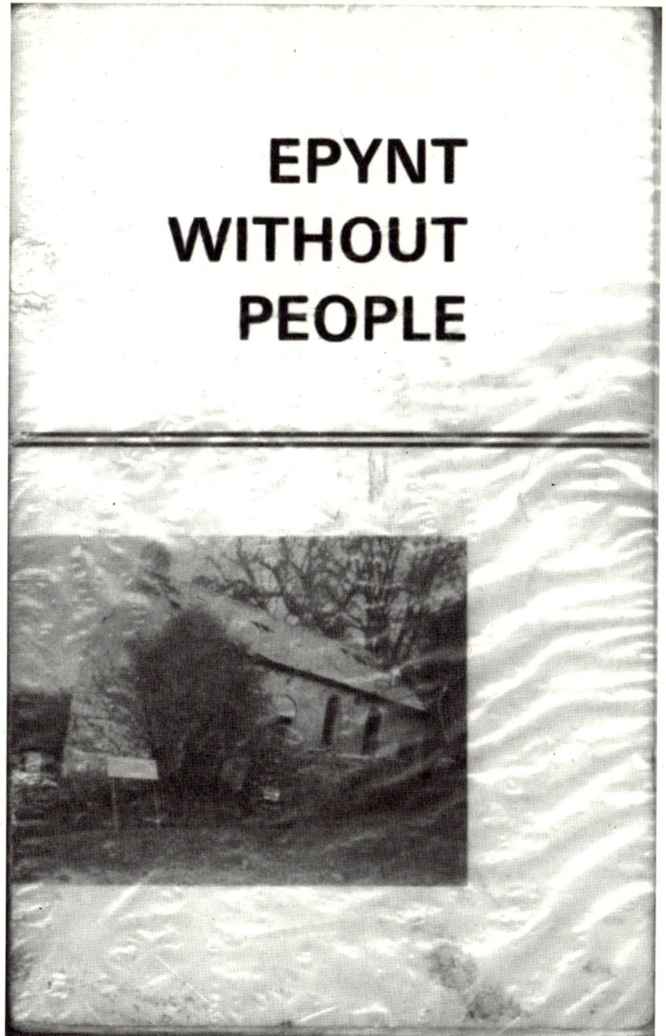
EPYNT
WITHOUT
PEOPLE

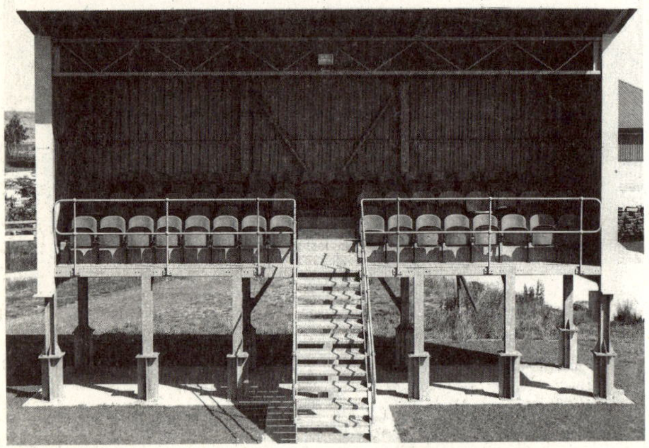

After some discussion, I am allowed to veer off the public roads. Epynt is synonymous with legendary crossings. An ancient trading route, and pilgrim's way, horses are alleged to be audible galloping and whining across the range. It was requisitioned in the 1930s, and the villagers and farmers moved away. The pamphlet is a painstaking litany of names.

I ask to see the buildings and am offered an escort around the site. I follow in my car, and am led to 'the village'. It is not the village I am expecting. It sits on the crest of a hill, amidst thousands of acres of undeveloped land. From afar it looks like a Disney rebuild, a quintessential European village, church resplendent with new red roof. We drive right in. There is a farm, a small *mairie*, a police station, some houses. It is all there, except the windows are unglazed and the front render of brick is missing. Apart from the church, the buildings are shells of breeze block and concrete. One of the houses is built as though its front wall has been sliced away, and a small sheltered auditorium stands opposite. The audience sit here to watch the performance of a perfect military house clearance.

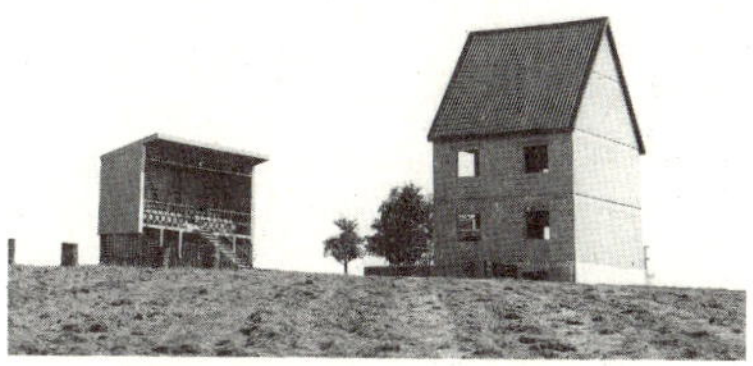

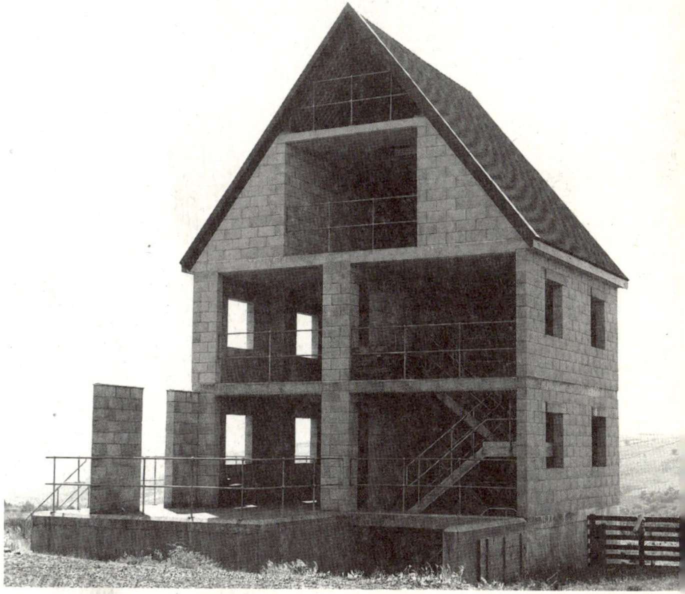

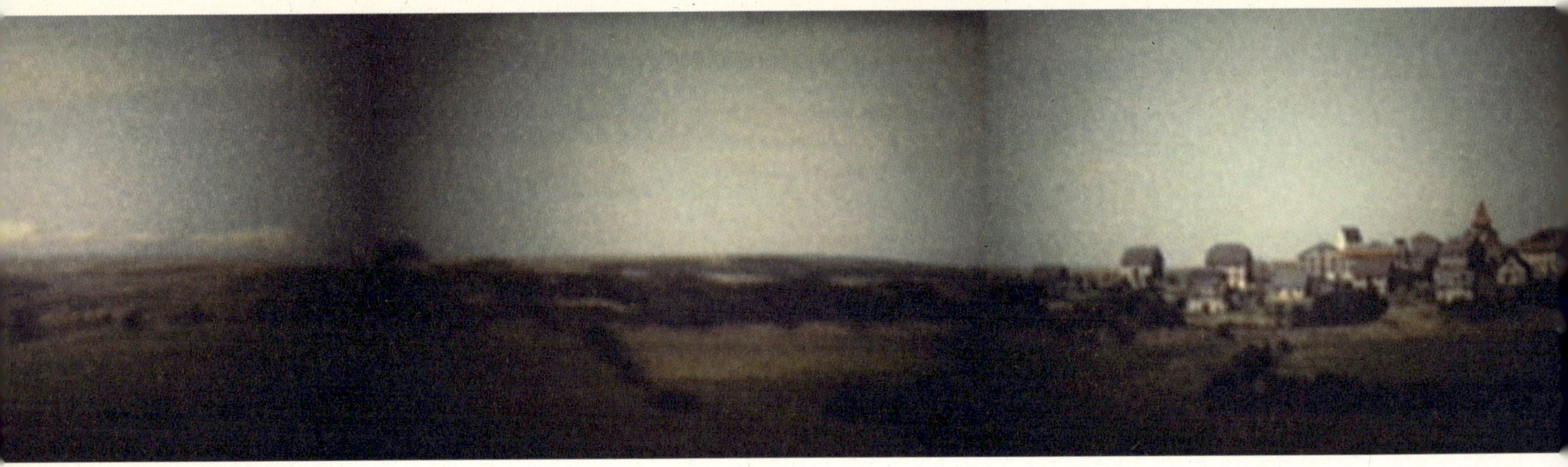

On the film footage, acres rush past, miles of brush and open skies. The foliag

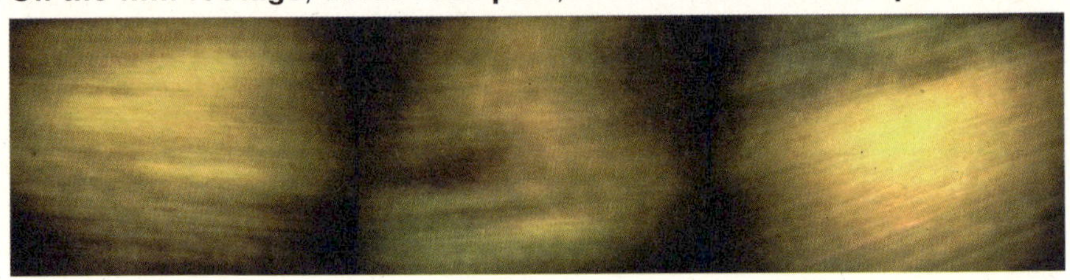

In true classical spirit, the church is the nerve centre of the village. Surveillance cameras film every sector and play back manœuvres on screens in the vestry. The church even has a graveyard, but the headstones are immaculate in every sense, and will never be inscribed. The village is designed for sniper practice and is built in a generic East European style. It was completed in 1988 and was feared to be obsolete before completion, but of course it has since been summoned into use.

The firing range is really too small to test many contemporary ballistics, so is in decreasing demand. There is an ecology centre, and the former pub has been restored – minus the bonhomie. You can't get a drink. But as a gesture of goodwill, the inhabited graveyard has also been restored a little, and the foundation walls of the collapsed church have been cleaned up. A greater sensitivity to local morale is being shown, and ex-inhabitants are now allowed back to tend their family graves. But the area can never be fully returned to civilian use as thousands of pounds of ammunition are embedded in the hillsides.

peculiar: it is neither farmed, nor wilderness.

The calm is charged with a feral energy. Like the reflexes we have hardly used, have half forgotten, regions of the brain and the soil quietly dedicated to emergency action.

There is a henge, far off in the distance. It turns out to be a circle of cars; painted white for target practice by overhead planes.

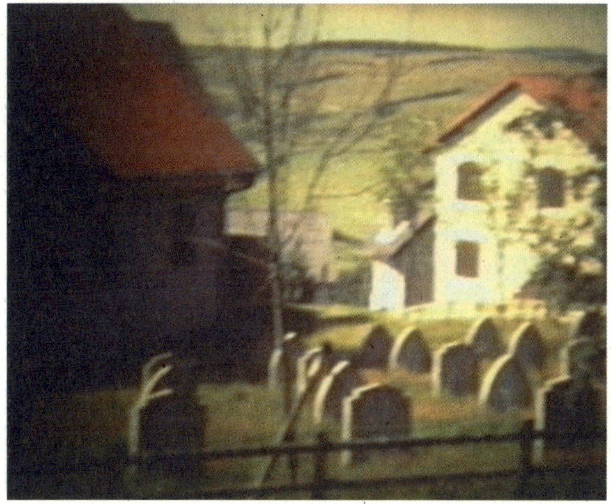

A good many meteorites fell in Europe, but the reaction against superstitions of the Middle Ages led the scientists of the day to such great scepticism that they refused to face facts ... In the eighteenth century the learned men of the day did not believe stones could fall from the skies, hence they affirmed they did not.

Encyclopaedia Americana

Three separate committees now exist in the US to raise public awareness about the likelihood of being hit by bolts from the blue. I'm reading news reports, trying to find something I heard on the radio, about a ship that capsized in the middle of the ocean, through nothing more than the unanimous resistance of the small fish in the nets. Whilst I'm searching I come across a story about video poker. There is something grand about this too, this playing off big numbers and statistics in the middle of the desert. If we play a bit with space-time-diffusion theory, the risk of being wiped out in an asteroid collision is about the same as dying in a plane crash, approximately 1 in 20,000. The odds were big enough for the lottery commission in Oregon to invest in research on how to reinstate their poker machines in such an event, to protect the millions they raise for the State. Of course if a really big asteroid did collide with earth, as they do every few million years, it would take 6 billion people with it. But then again, it may be a small one, and just add a little edge to playing with the odds.

The whole city floats on a sleek frisson of anxiety and promise that those of us addicted to such distraction must otherwise induce by motion or medication. And win or lose, you always have that instant of genuine, justifiable hope. Even though we know the rules governing random events are always overtaken by the law of large numbers, there is always that window of opportunity, that statistical crazy zone, before this happens, when anything can happen. And what's more, if you win, you win. You can take it home. You cannot be deemed unworthy after the fact as we all were in Washington, where we all played our heart out and never had a fucking chance.

Dave Hickey

Islands, mountains, lost cities: nineteenth-century fiction corrupted these landscapes into the destinations of buried treasure. Something of the pilgrimage remains, because these geographies are part of the imagery of Utopia, or its relics. The journey is directed inwards as well as out into geographical space to get at the gold. At the lower end of the market, in the Penny Dreadfuls, pirates and gold-diggers come in as anti-heroes, maverick journeymen who transcend the class limitations of an old Europe, and inhabit worlds of adventure, eroticism, stealth and bounty. A place where adventure could invent its own laws.

For two months, 150 workmen laboured to build the 1,000-foot long, 500-foot wide lamasery, with its deep flights of marble stairs and huge patio, broad terraces, rich gardens, lily-coated pools, and main building influenced by art deco and Frank Lloyd Wright.

Hollywood has come back to the Tibetan Mountains, to Shangri-La. The film that coined the term, Frank Capra's 1937 movie *The Lost Horizon*, was the most expensive ever made, a budget to match its aspiration. Shangri-La is a European enclave, high up in the Himalayas, 'uncontaminated' by the outside world, save for art treasures, books and antiques. The lamasery is a mansion complex , running on the principles of modesty, courtesy and an abundance of time. Local culture assimilates peacefully in return for benign snippets of European learning. The (English) hero is kidnapped and air-lifted to Paradise from the troubled Chinese city of Baskul, where he was co-ordinating the evacuation of 'white people' from a local political uprising. The mountains form a 'hedge of inaccessible purity', they are even filled with gold. He is enchanted by the vision. But when he decides to leave after a crisis of faith, it is on foot, and he is pitched against every hazard the terrain can muster. It is via this earthly passage that he must re-enter Shangri-La when his faith is restored. The original nitrate film has deteriorated – though the soundtrack is intact. When you watch the movie on video, sections of the film are frozen in stasis while the spoken story unfolds.

Other material may still exist.
Our search for the missing footage goes on ...
National Center for Film & Video Preservation,
American Film Institute

Sir E cares very little for the scientific work but is eyeing the expdn. more in the light of a commercial venture . . .

Frank Hurley

We had pierced the veneer of outside things . . . heard the text that Nature renders

Ernest Shackleton

The Kodak Vest Vintage Camera, that may or may not have been recently discovered alongside Mallory's remains by climbers, sponsored by TV station PBS, has been described as the 'Holy Grail,' with the possibility that the first photograph taken at the summit of the world may yet be developed....' Shackleton also understood the necessity of pictures. Some suggested that he had a naive and unfounded fantasy of finding buried treasure on his polar missions. Others suggested that he knew that the real treasure was to be found in media rights and pictures. Empire, science and spirituality were pretexts for drumming up sponsorship to get there, but the pictures would mean cash on return. He registered the ITA (Imperial Trans Arctic) Film Syndicate Ltd and employed the highly respected cameraman Frank Hurley to document the mission, and led a competitive tender to newspapers before his departure. 'The mercenary side of a polar expedition is absorbing. Any day you may see Sir Ernest – always alone – taxiing from one newspaper office to another. He is trying to arrange the best terms and it is going to be a battle royal for both the news and pictorial rights'. (*London Mail* January 1914) So with the scramble for old pictures comes the rumour of new Hollywood releases; one, maybe two movies each explorer.

ART TREASURES SAFE. 1-2-43.
300FT. DEEP IN CAVES.

PASSED BY CENSOR.

THE ART TREASURES OF THE NATIONAL GALLERY, NOW HOUSED IN AIR CONDITIONED SUB-TERRANEAN CAVES IN WHICH THE TEMPERATURE AND HUMIDITY ARE SCIENTIFICALLY CONTROLLED ARE BEING MAINTAINED IN SUCH PERFECT CONDITION THAT EXPERTS ARE WONDERING WHAT WILL HAPPEN WHEN THEY ARE BROUGHT BACK TO LONDON AFTER THE WAR. THE PICTURES ARE SAFELY STORED IN AN UNDERGROUND WORKING WITH BETWEEN 200 AND 300FT., OF ROCK COVER, WHICH IS IMPREGNABLE TO AIR ATTACK. . NOTHING BUT AN EARTH-QUAKE COULD HARM THESE TREASURES AND THE STAFF LIKE THE CREW OF A SHIP, GIVE CEASELESS ATTENTION TO THE MACHINERY, WHICH CONTROLLS THE TEMPERATURE AND A QUARTER OF A MILE OF MINATURE RAILWAY.

I manage to get the Internet, with its great search engines, to locate the Treasure Mountain for me. McAlpine is mining it now, and I speak to the manager on the line. He is the former owner and on his way out of the job. He tells me that the National Art Collection was stored in the Mountain during World War II. It is winter now, and he advises me to wait until spring for a visit. The roads are treacherous and the caverns are very wet.

'National' in this context transpires to be British. The paintings made their way through these winding lanes from Trafalgar Square, and spent the wartime safely ensconced under hundreds of feet of rock. Lloyd George and the then Director of the National Gallery, Sir Kenneth Clark, recommended Manod for safekeeping. A report was commissioned and next to his signature Churchill wrote, 'Bury the paintings in the bowels of the earth, but never let a painting leave this island.'

Blaenau Ffestiniog – the nearest town to the Manod quarry – lies in the heart of the Snowdonia National Park. A great red circle of exemption has been drawn round it, and the slate has been blasted from the mountainside. Vast sheets of slate and shingle embrace the houses built in bolt straight terraces, sheer inclines rising from the garden walls. Manod is a few miles south, and is surrounded by a mountain panorama. The summit is razed back to steel grey shards, but the aspect is one of tranquillity and repose. It is not until you near the summit that the birdsong mingles with the electronic signals of reversing trucks. When I look into the archive in the National Gallery, it is rich with images, reports, dockets and letters all carefully, chronologically ordered. The first file is the feasibility study: tentative letters and communiqués.

The site visits were obviously cherished – amidst the letters from directors to ministers to mine-owners are chitties for cups of tea, pleasant stays in guest houses, shots of the local scenery and stunning mountainside views. Sir Kenneth Clark spent most of his war years in the nearby Italianate village of Portmeirion. His frequent visits to Manod, he said later, were because of his love of the Welsh landscape.

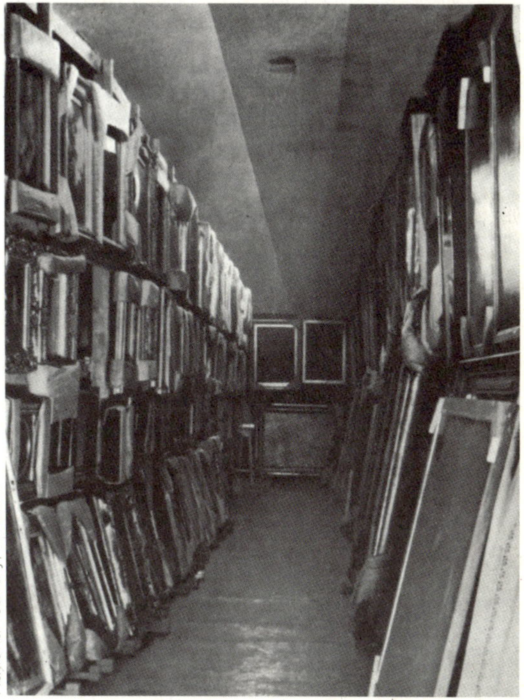

National Gallery, London

In the next file I find images of works: customised tracks running into the mountainside with truckloads of canvases, winding lamplight tunnels, racks of Old Masters hung inside vast chambers top to tail like post apocalyptic Salons.

It was said that *Charles the First on Horseback* and *The Raising of Lazarus* caused the most difficulty on their way into the mountain.

The caverns housed the entire collection – it was imperative to keep it together. Even the library and a temporary conservation unit worked from the quarry, in carefully ventilated chambers.

Come springtime I am able to visit. The mouth of the quarry is shaped like a grotto. We carry out the journey by the light of a single lamp. Now the walls are stripped and damp; water courses in as the dynamite works closer. The caverns are falling in. The brick chambers are all intact, save for their ceilings – so that the vastness of the caverns above and the scale of the operation is unveiled. It is very dark, and monotone, but it is as if a chromatic after-image still lingers. Outlines are etched on the wall, everywhere are remains. With its complex electrical systems and security offices, it is suddenly a very twentieth-century phenomenon, and the literary genre has shifted to political thriller.

The Ministry of Works – later the Department of the Environment – kept the site in full working order way beyond the war. Though the paintings made their way back to London during VE week, it wasn't until 1983, after a protracted court battle, that the Manager regained possession. When journalists and locals were allowed in for the first time on 24 September 1983, OHMS labels were still gummed to the walls, placing works by Michelangelo, Vermeer, Rembrandt, Hobbema and Rubens. Scanning the inventory of the collection: Claude, Poussin, Titian, Botticelli ... the 'National' denomination clearly denotes ownership over authorship. Strains of Bach, Beethoven and Mozart were heard at daily concerts through the emptied galleries at Trafalgar Square during the evacuation, as an anthem to the tenacity of British cultural life. The return of the paintings to London was an exercise in triumphalism. The collection returned intact.

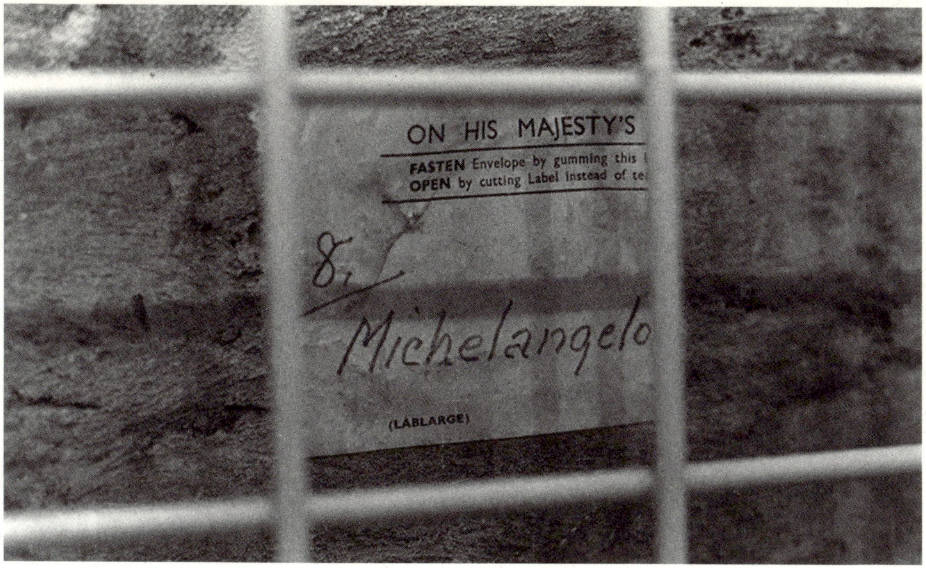

Nigel Hughes

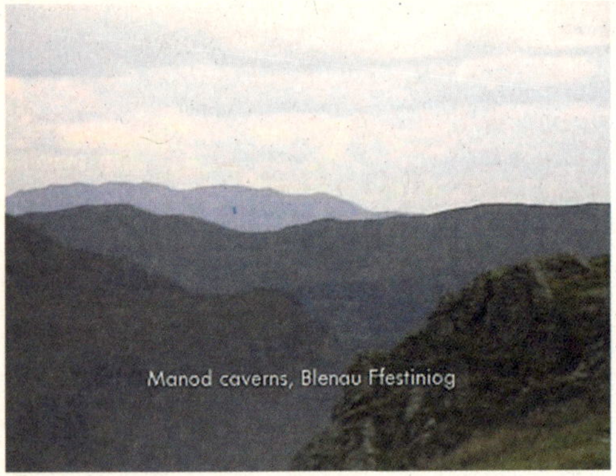

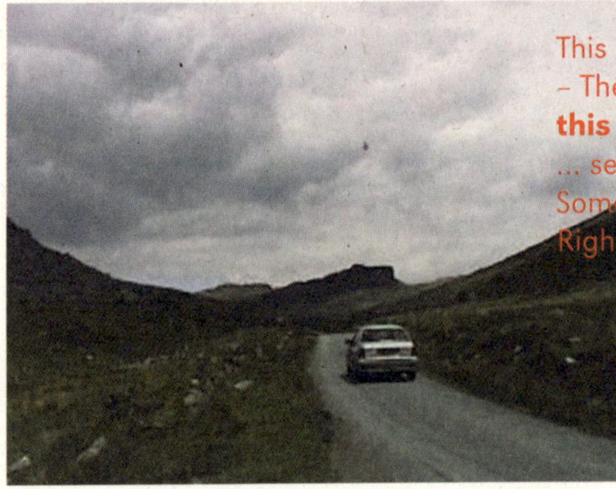

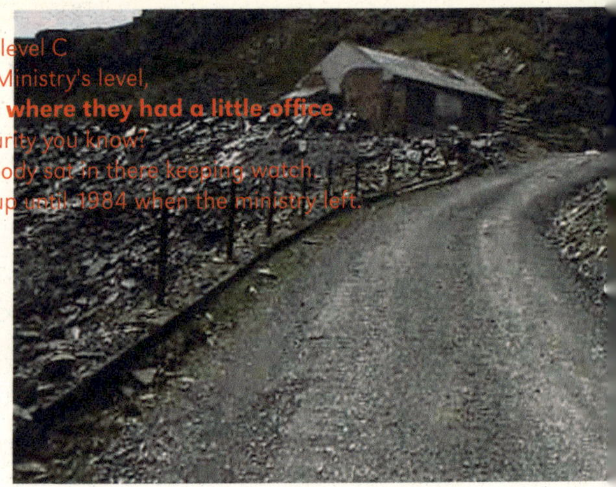

This is level C
– The Ministry's level,
this is where they had a little office
... security you know?
Somebody sat in there keeping watch.
Right up until 1984 when the ministry left.

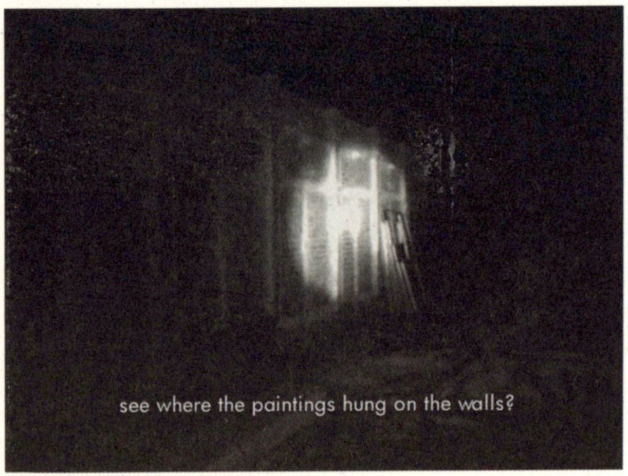

You can see parts of the ventilation system
... they say the paintings kept better in here
... than the gallery. It's hard to walk in here lets go on to the next.
I think I'm right,
I've looked at the model.
They call this chamber 2.
They kept the most prized paintings in here.
see where the paintings hung on the walls?

Where the individual paintings were attached?
This leads us to the next chamber...
These rooms would have had ceilings on the top up there ... the roof bolts
This is glass from the conservation department.
There was a collapse once. A fall of slate from the cavern.
For a moment they thought they had lost everything
but it turned out to be quite light

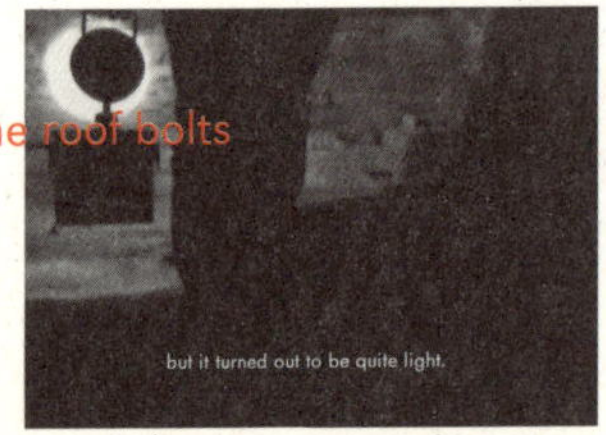

We have such extreme weather here,
we have to work fast now to make up for the slowness of winter ...
We will be working hard around here
– it won't be safe to come in at all soon.
The smell is the magazines: we've been working with the dynamite.
This is the way to the caverns
round here
where they kept the paintings.
You can see where they laid rails to transport the paintings
it's about a quarter of a mile or so inside ...
The first chamber is just through here now.

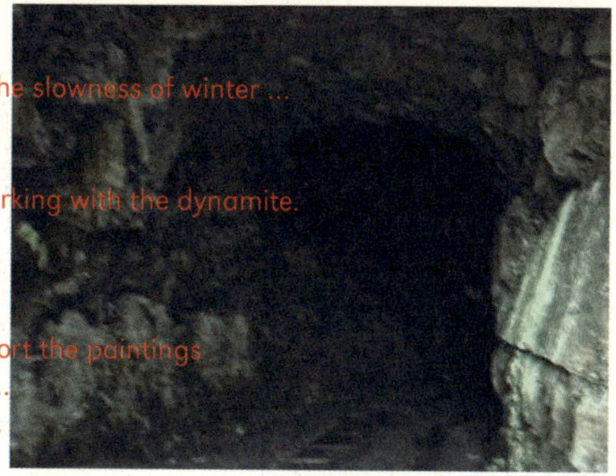

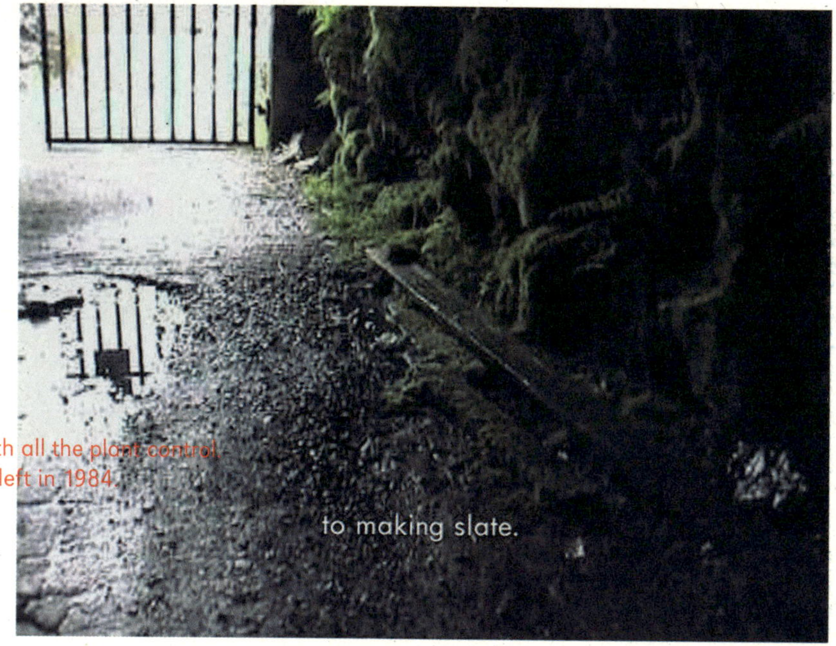

and the paintings were saved
... it's obviously collapsing now.
We're blasting above.
I'm sure it was incredible when it was dry,
when the ventilation was working, and the light
– when the actual paintings were hanging there
... like something out of like one of these spy thrillers.
I think there were a couple of thousand pictures
they built six of those units and another further down here with all the plant control.
The units were ready, warm and ventilated until the last man left in 1984,
just in case.
The owner took the ministry to court to get them out
– so now it's back to making slate.

Another mountain in the range has since been hollowed out in an amazing scheme. It has been named 'Electric Mountain' – and a huge water-driven turbine generator creates electricity; tonnes of water descend hundreds of metres to provide full output in as little as 16 seconds. This mountain has 16km of underground tunnels, and has been landscaped to cover its internal workings. It is a strange, Sisyphean task – when the water has descended the turbines are reversed and it is pumped back to the reservoir at the top, usually at night when electricity is cheaper. (It is really designed for surges in demand, when millions of TV viewers in English cities switch on their kettles at the end of football matches and soap operas).

The Americans have pioneered the Global Positioning System – a network of satellites that provides the Pentagon with constant 24 bit graphics of every metre of the planet, as well as a 3-D grid reference for anyone in the vicinity. The system simultaneously looks in on Earth and out to space, and so our anxiety of orientation and territory enters into the realm of science fiction. (In the Sudan, when the news broke of Americans walking on the moon, the country entered a week long period of mourning).

Although astronauts have flown 384,000km to set up bases on the moon, no-one has set foot on the deepest ocean floor, 11km down.

The modern pleasure is always free and fearless. Brightly exhilarating and wholly unreflective so the painter feels that his foreground may be more consistently animated by sportsmen rather than a hermit, and our mountain society in general goes to the mountains not to fast but to feast, and leaves their glaciers covered with chicken bones and eggshells.

John Ruskin

… The patchwork continuity of an earth seen in this style undermines the concept of nationhood which relies upon the cultural idea of an island – undermines too the notion of the book as an island. Narrative is no longer held within the determining contours of land space.

Gillian Beer

Whilst I am collecting and shooting film footage of casinos, mountains and ships at sea, I e-mail a request to all the local newspapers for coastal regions in the UK, asking their readers to contact me with any films or photographs they may have of the ocean. Someone sends me a video – two hours of transposed film footage shot from the deck of her husband's boat over a 20 year period, circumnavigating the globe as a merchant seaman. As with my footage, light has leaked in and exposed the film, especially at the join of each three minute reel. They are scratched, punched and marked, with hasty notes scribbled on the leaders, and anticipate the stories of collisions and contest. And like all the landscape footage I have, the relentless searching for the picture frame, and scanning away at the horizon seems to invite the addition of a subtitle. The details that would explain his own story are edited out in the reflex that seeks broad landscapes and panoramic views. Amongst the papers she sends me is a small book, handwritten in pencil. It is a moving testimonial, written by her husband, when his boat was capsized during the war.

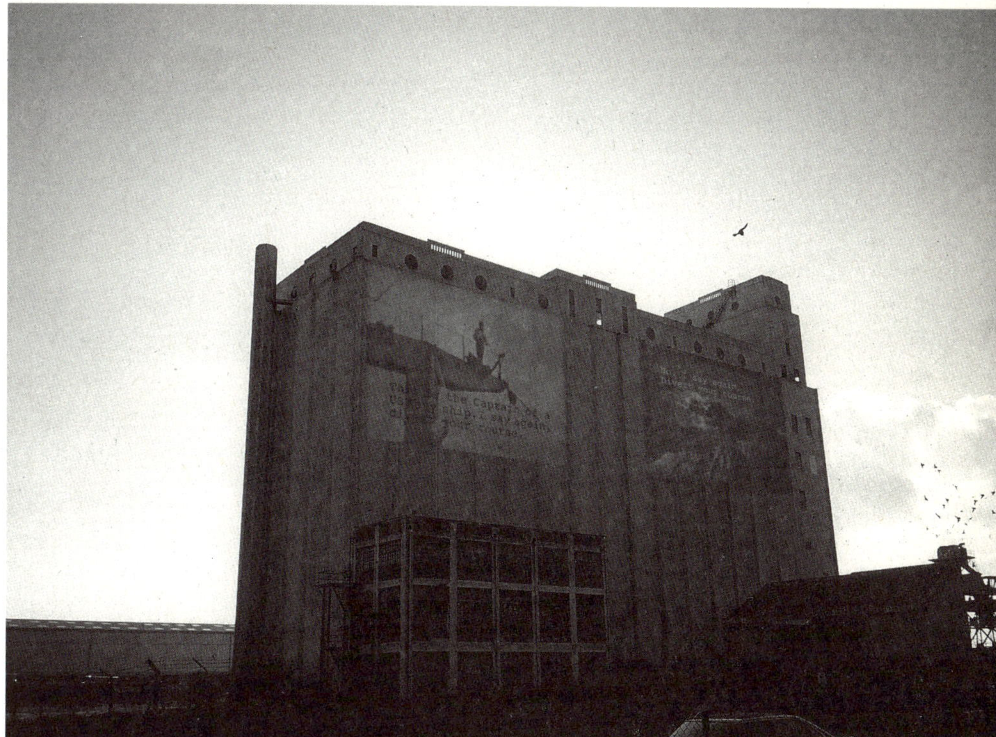

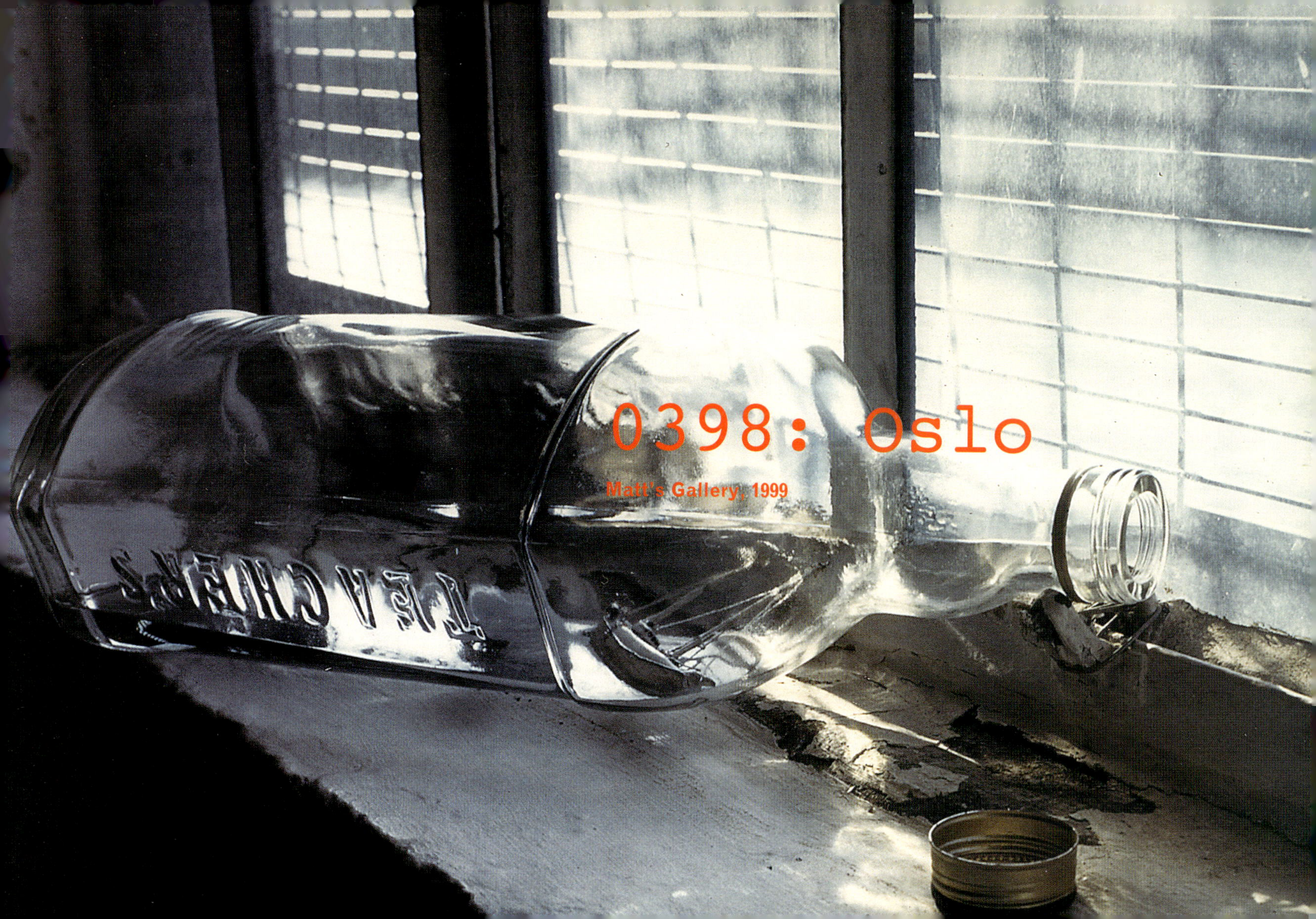

0398: Oslo

Matt's Gallery, 1999

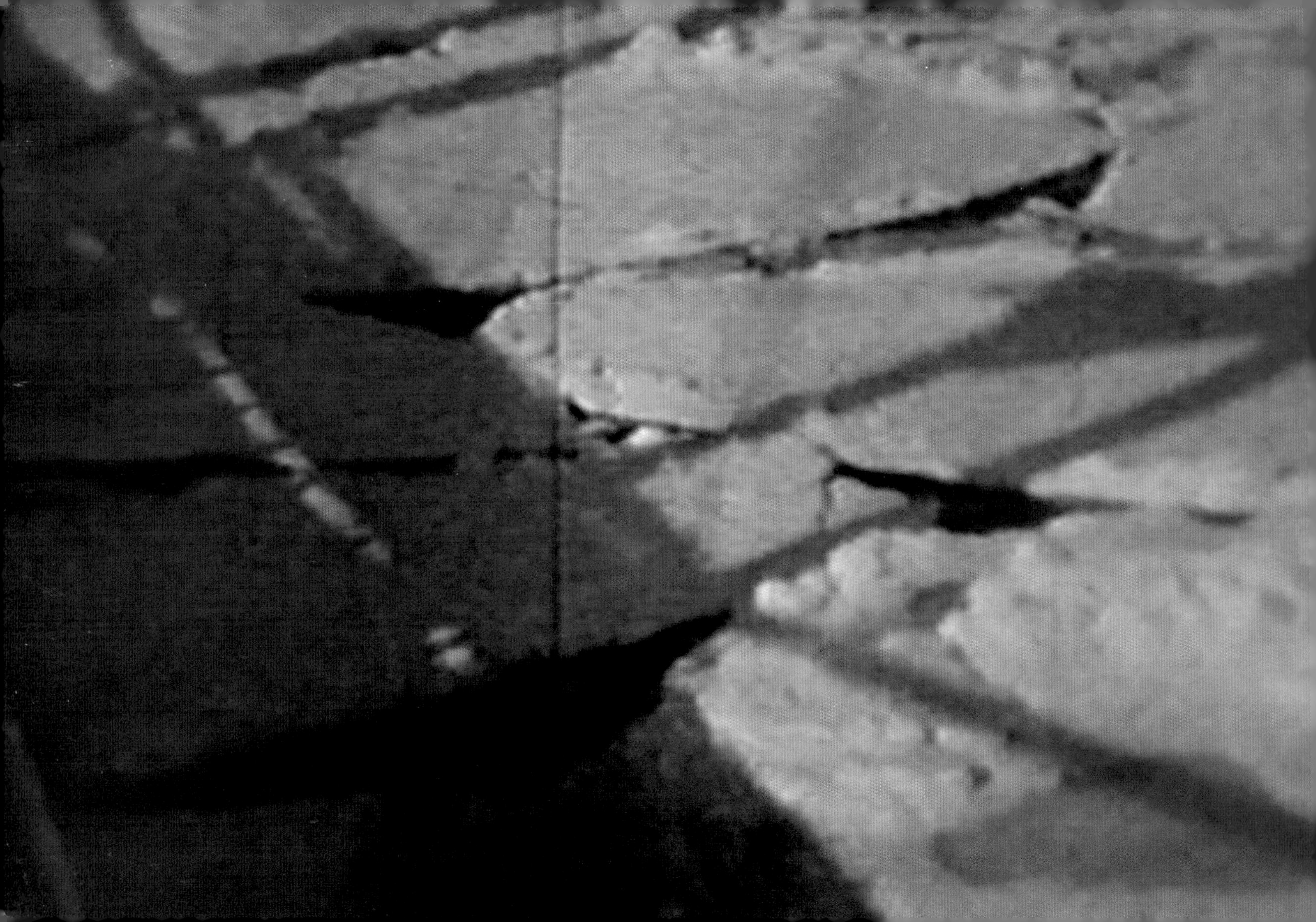

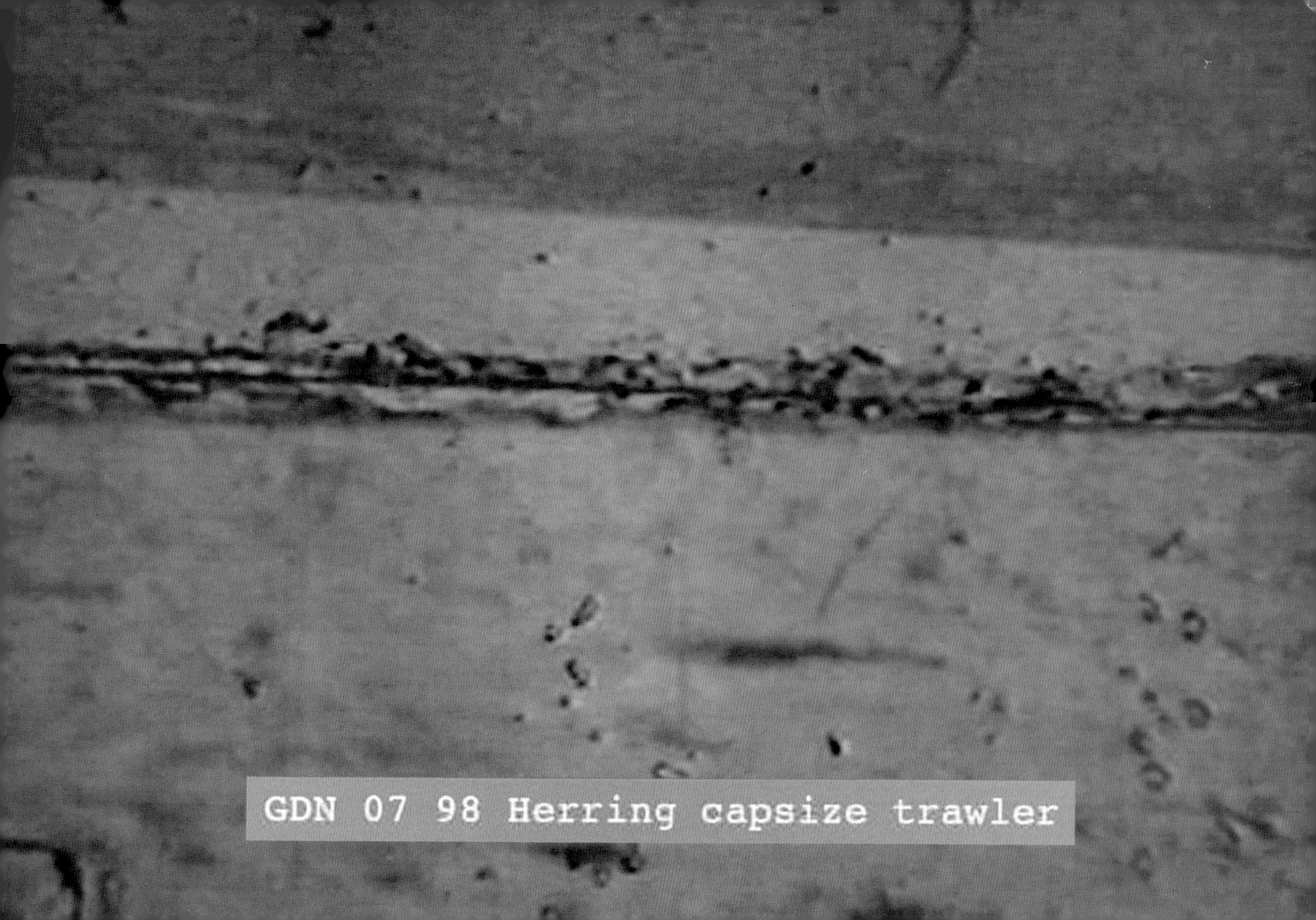
GDN 07 98 Herring capsize trawler

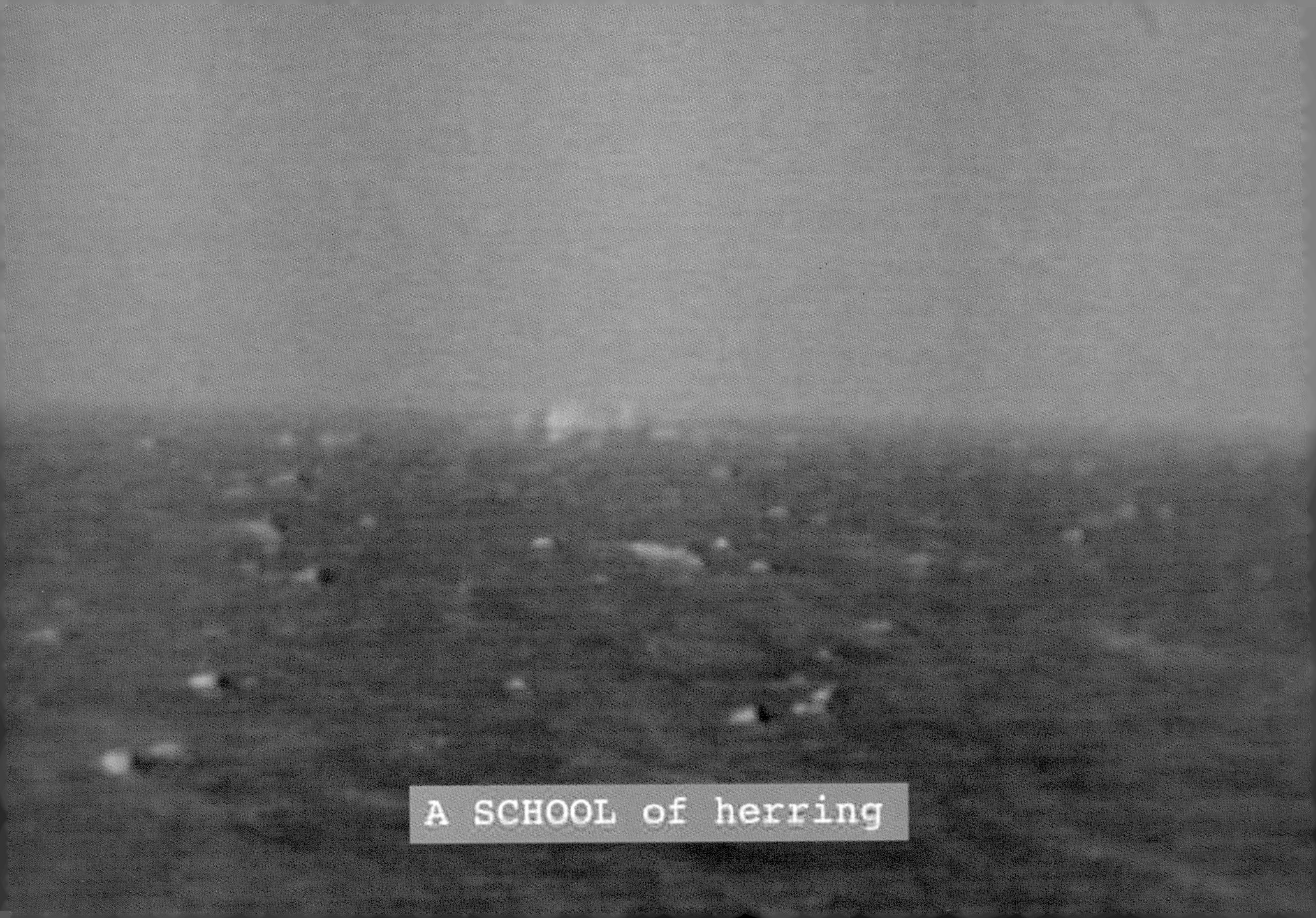

A SCHOOL of herring

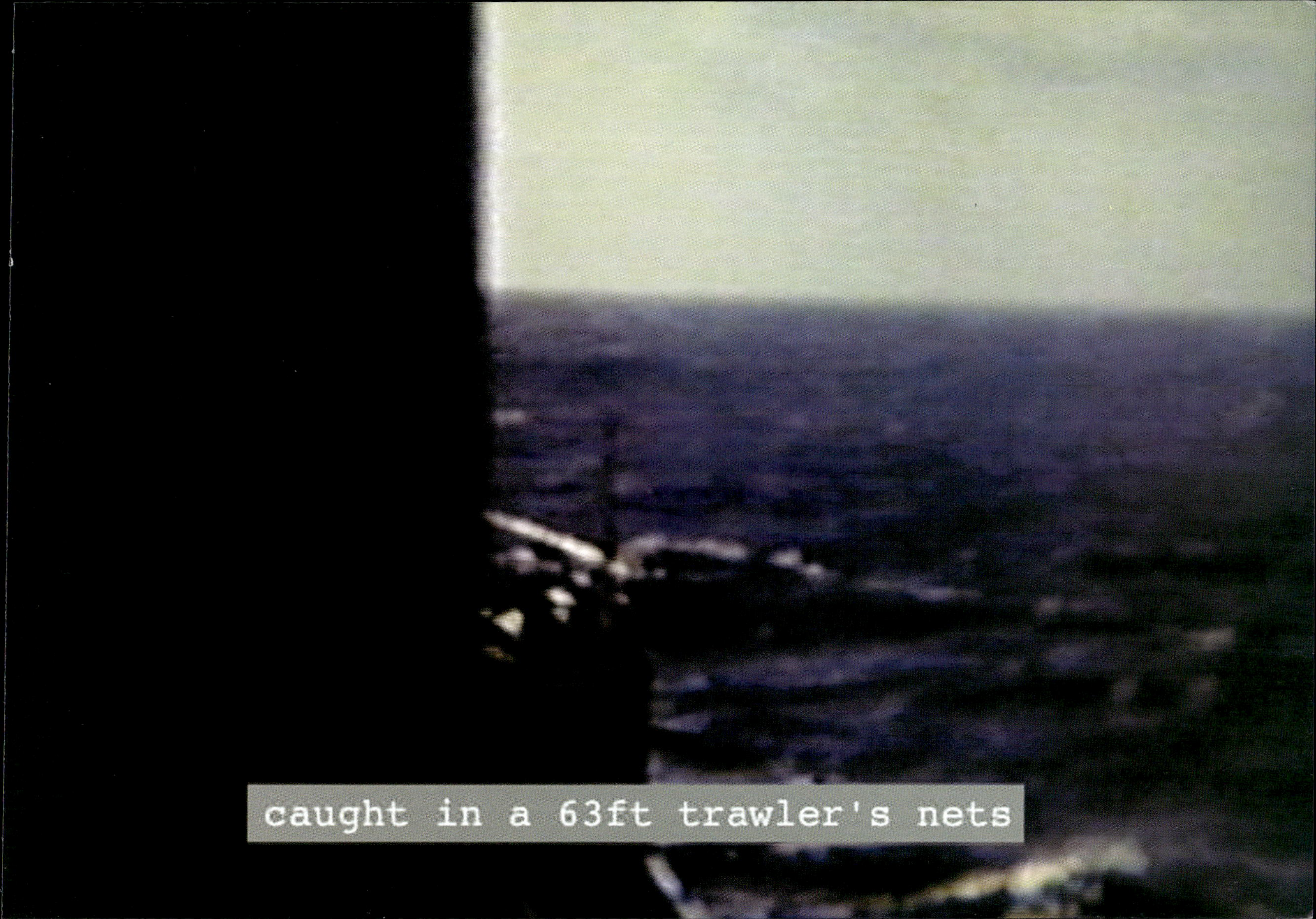
caught in a 63ft trawler's nets

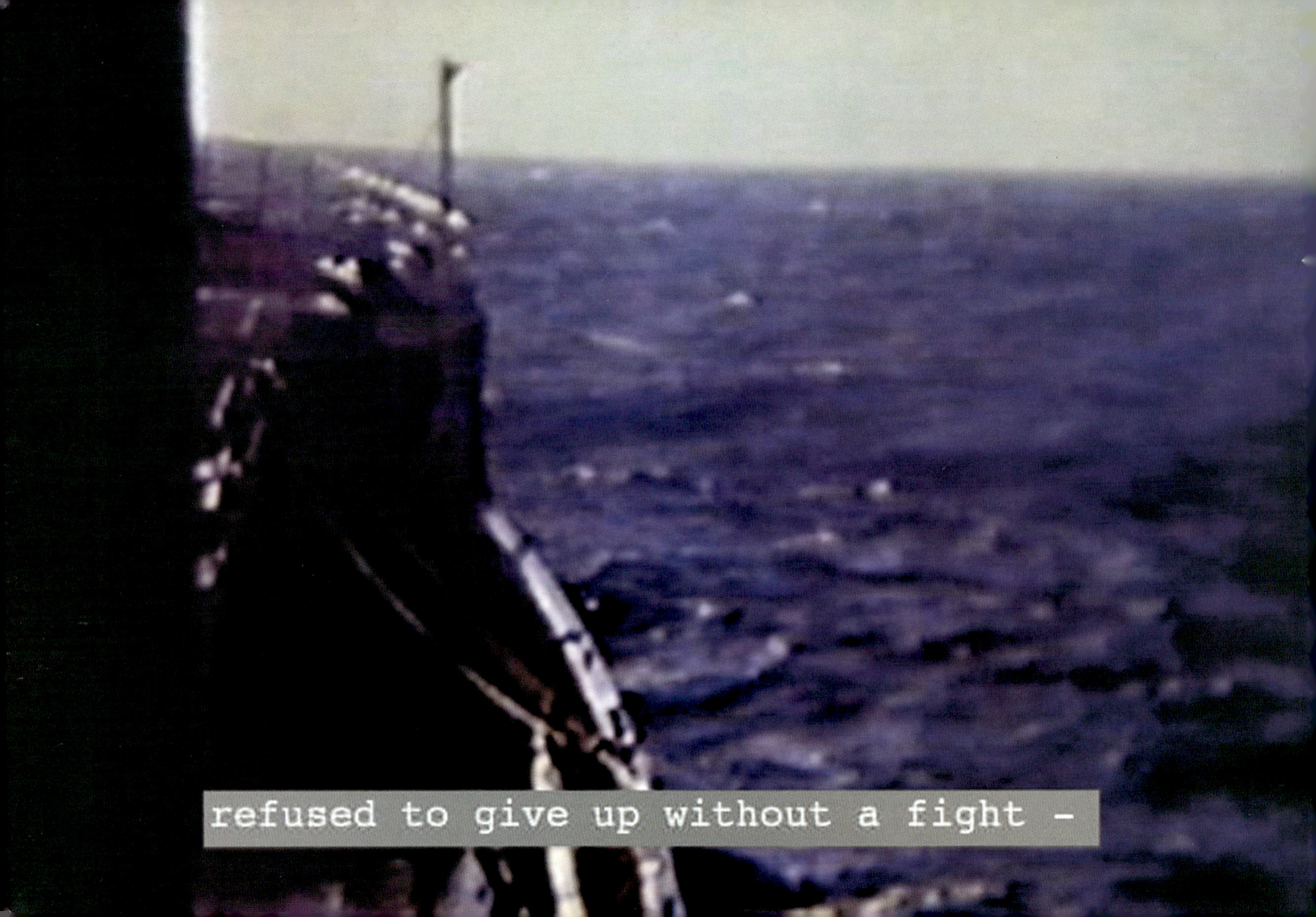
refused to give up without a fight -

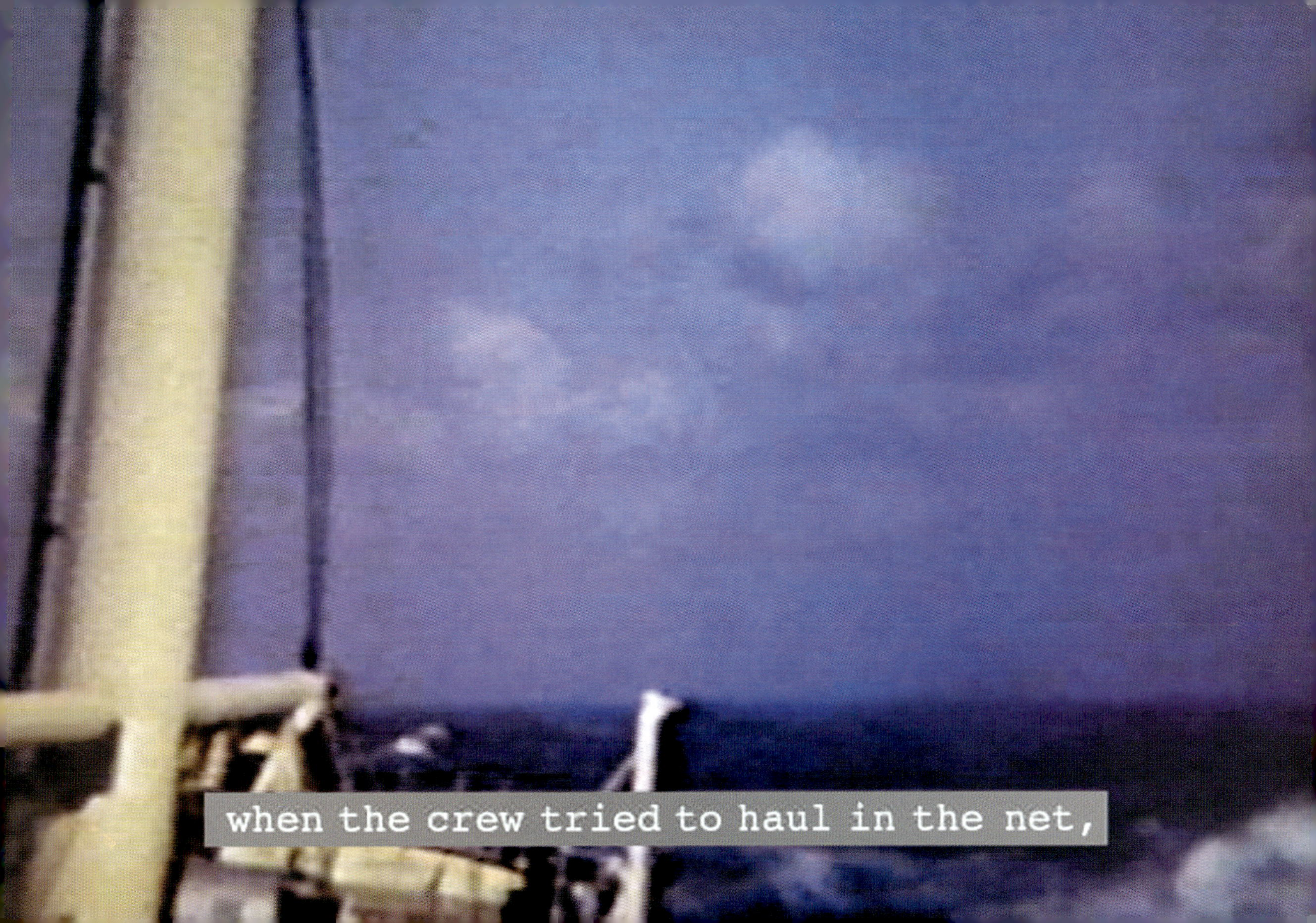
when the crew tried to haul in the net,

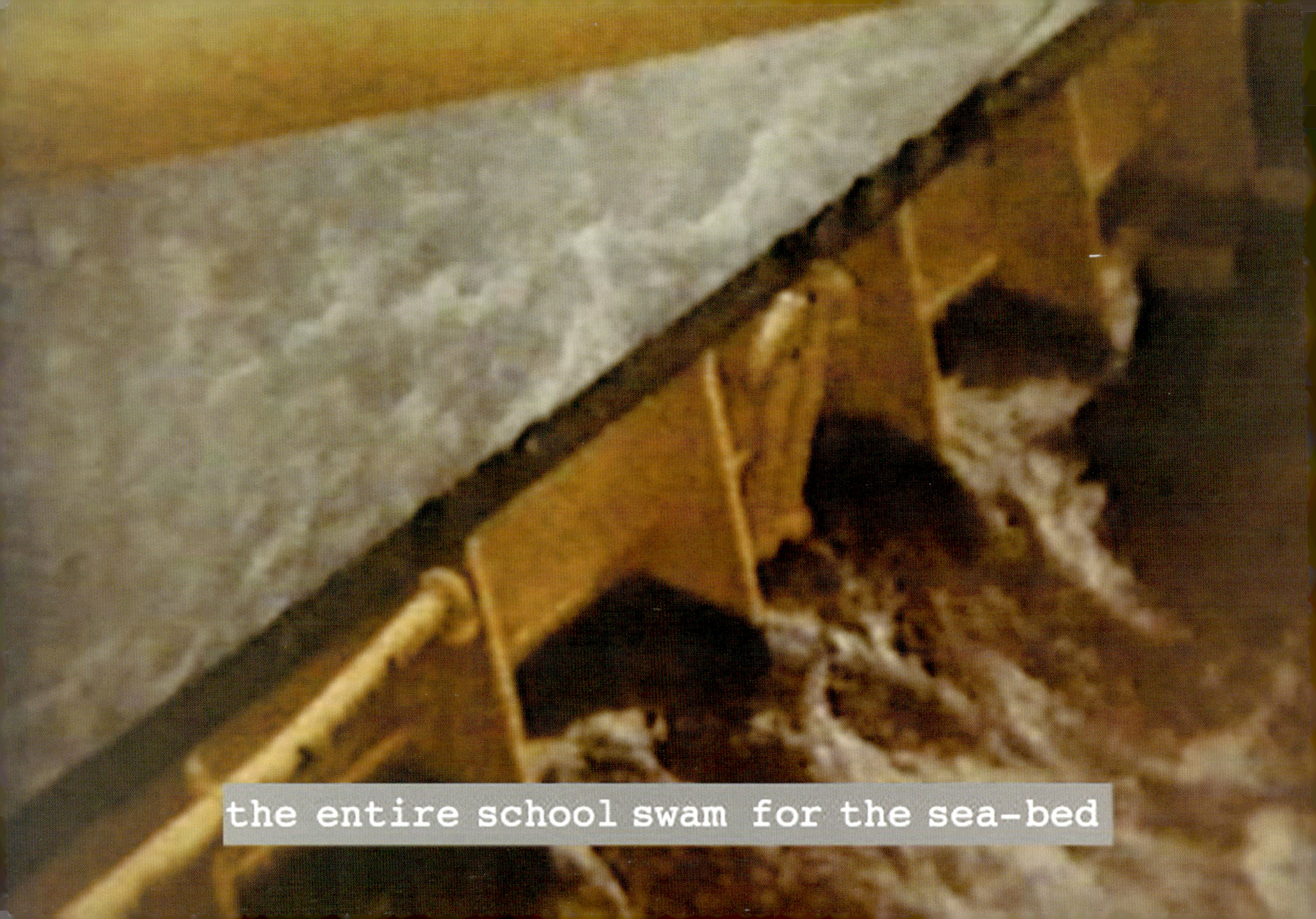
the entire school swam for the sea-bed

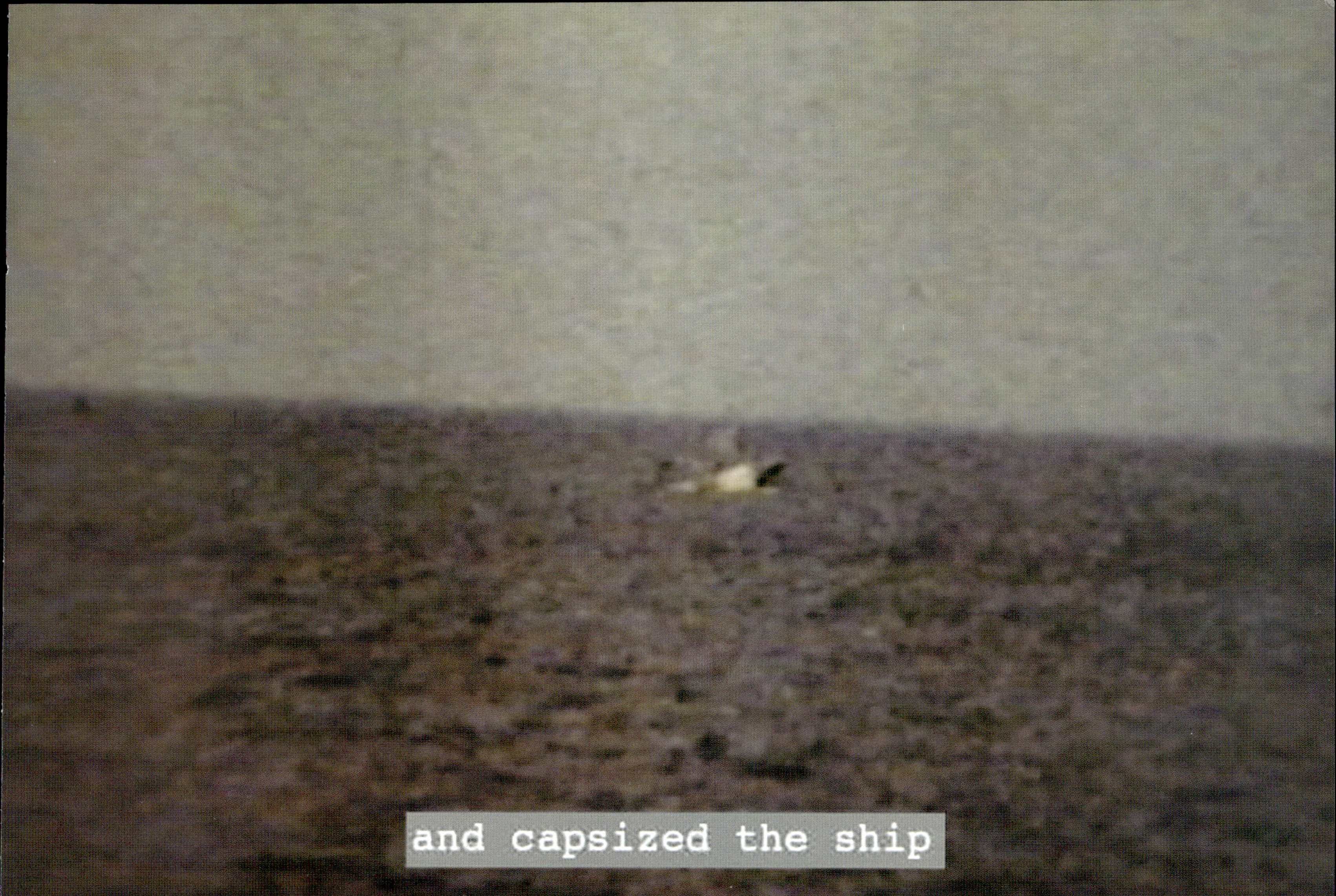
and capsized the ship

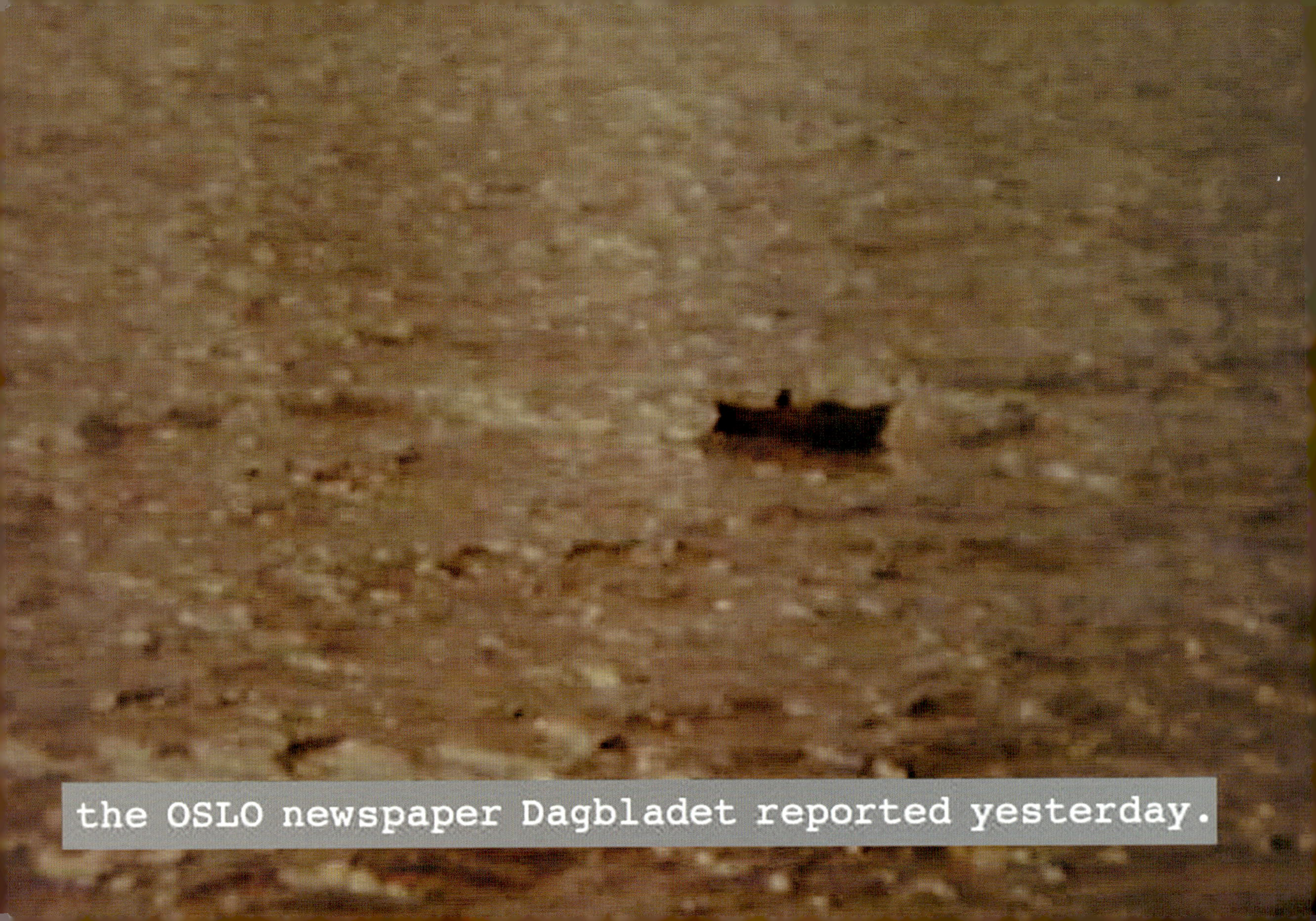
the OSLO newspaper Dagbladet reported yesterday.

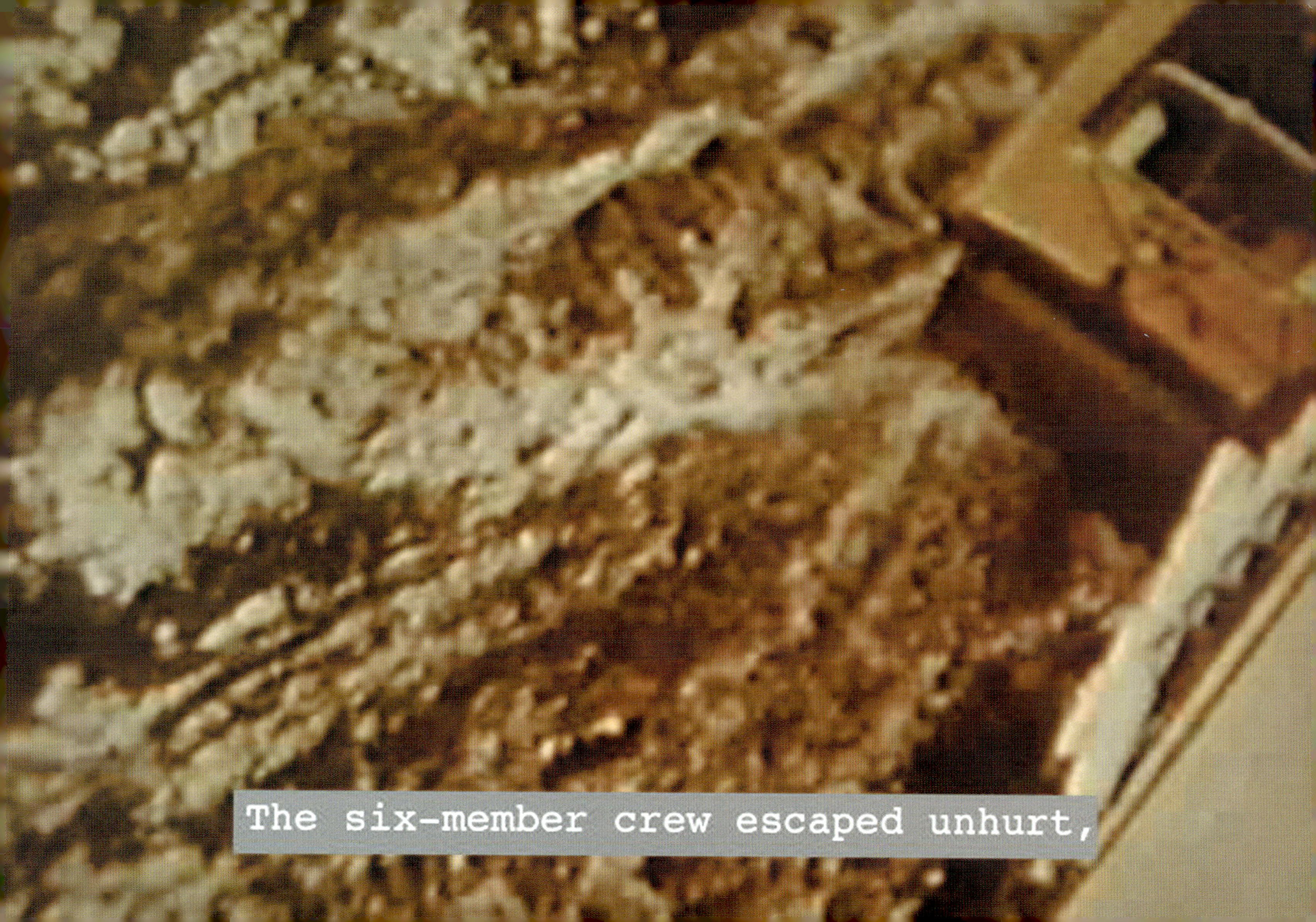
The six-member crew escaped unhurt,

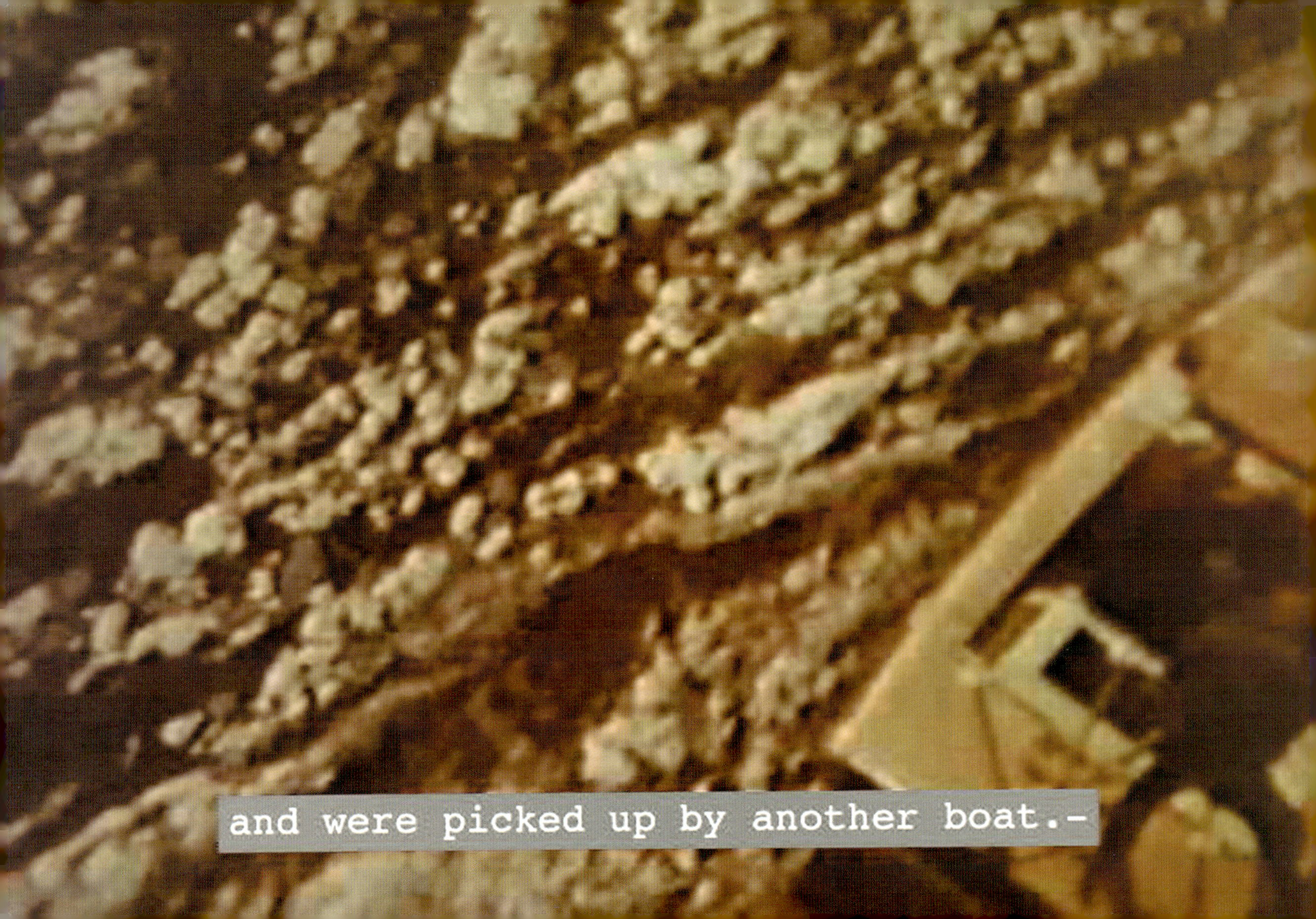
and were picked up by another boat.-

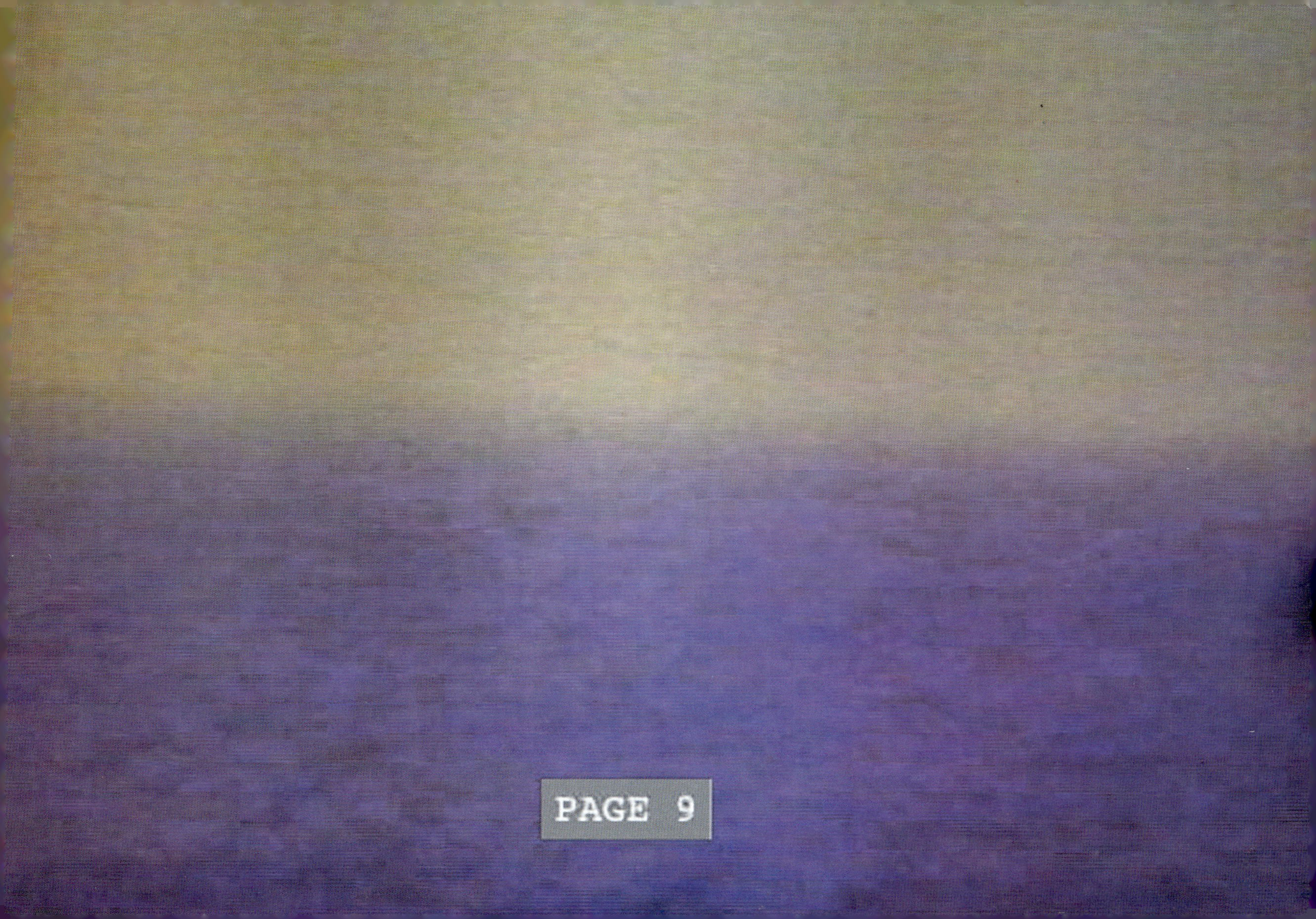
PAGE 9

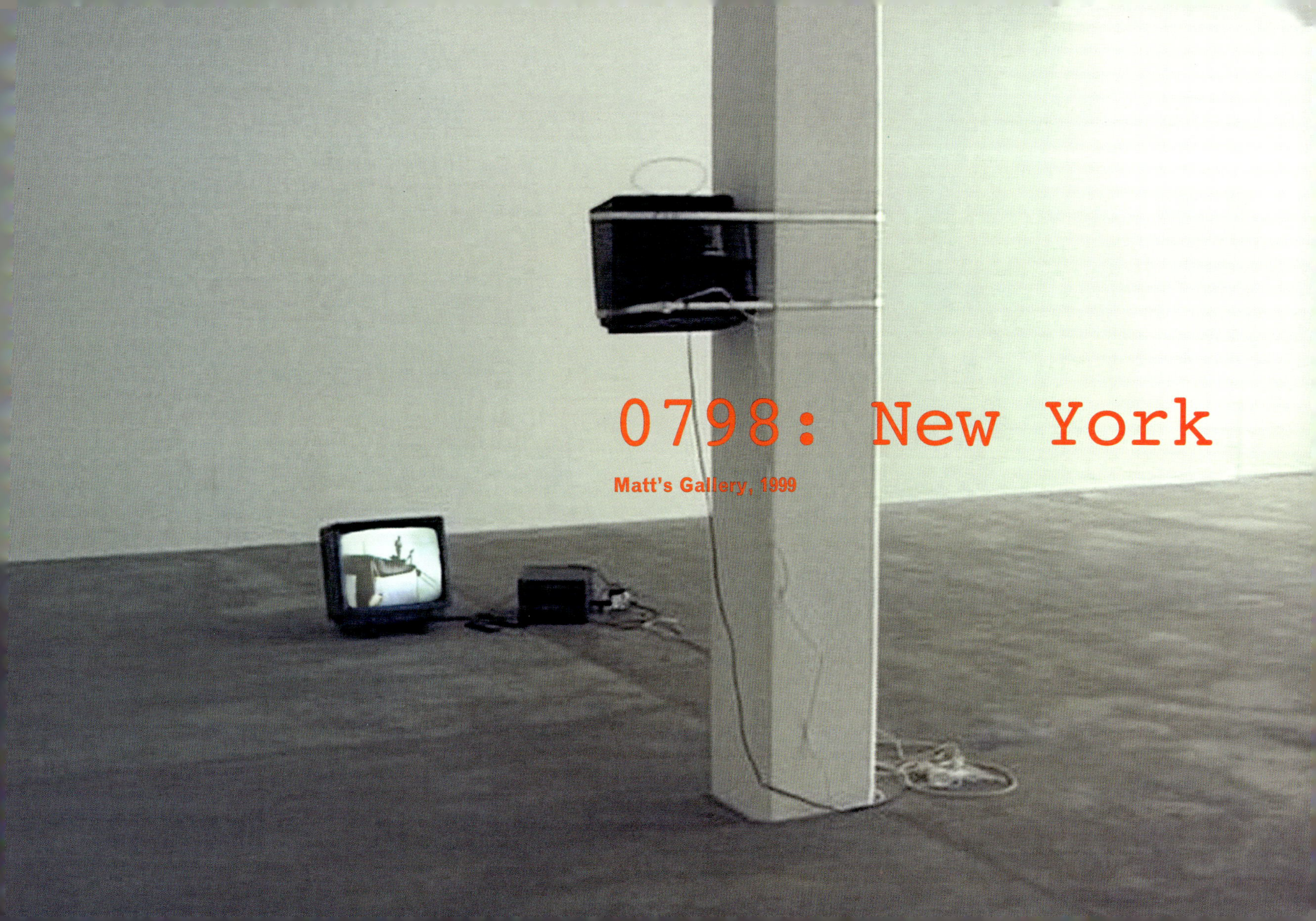
0798: New York
Matt's Gallery, 1999

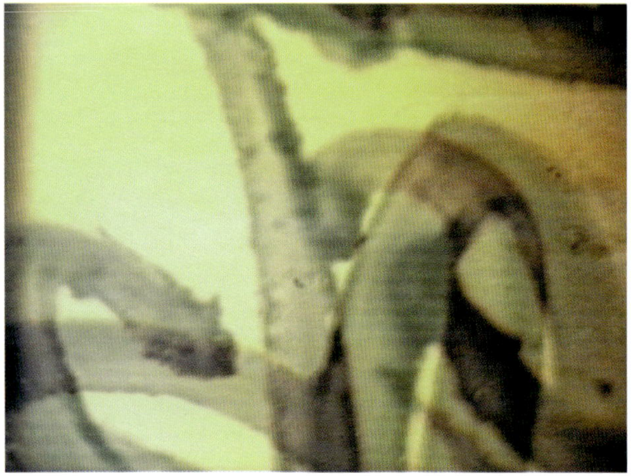

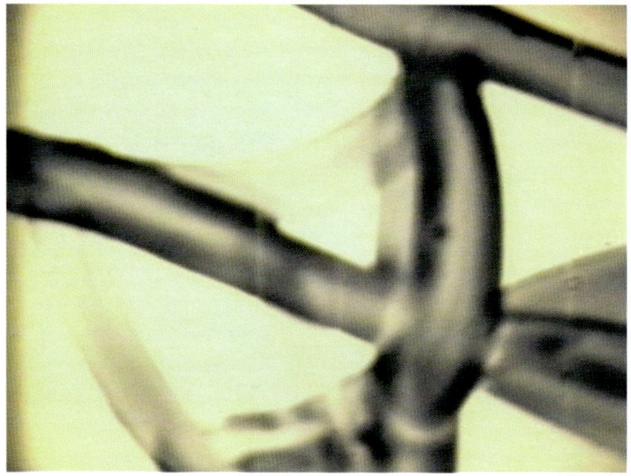

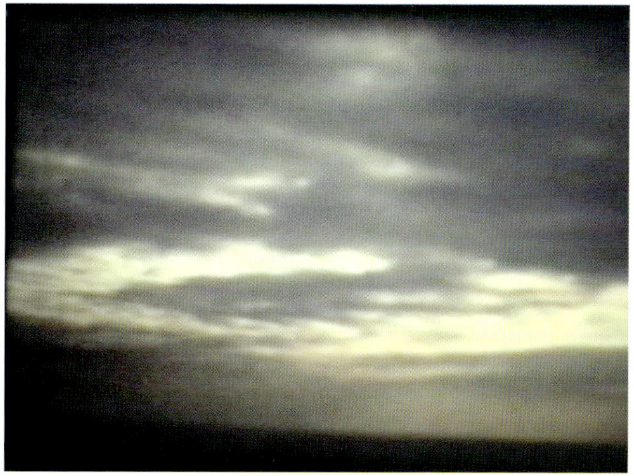

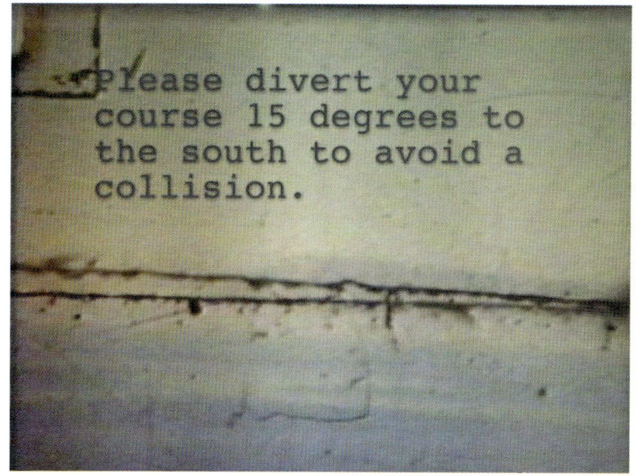
Please divert your course 15 degrees to the south to avoid a collision.

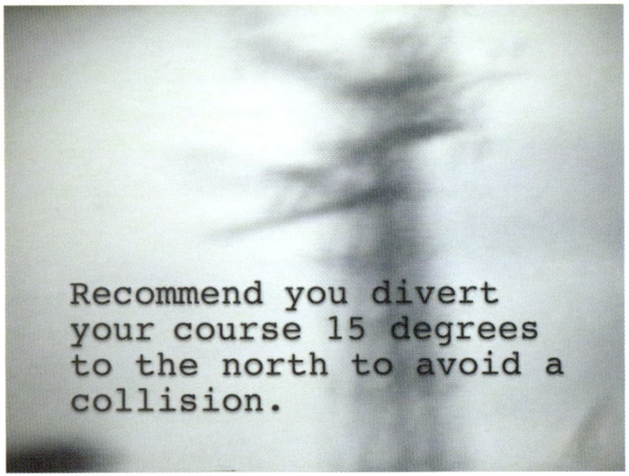
Recommend you divert your course 15 degrees to the north to avoid a collision.

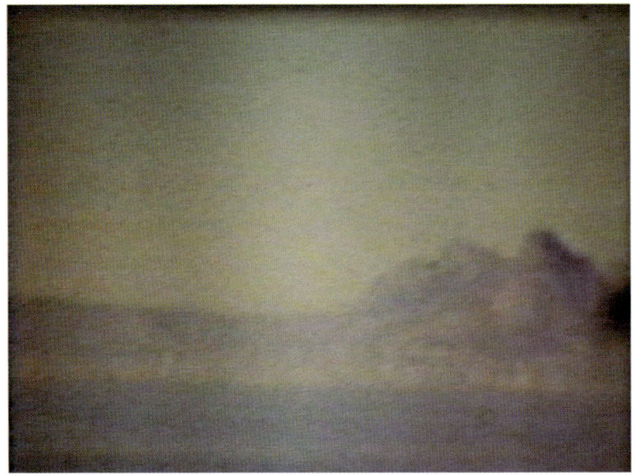

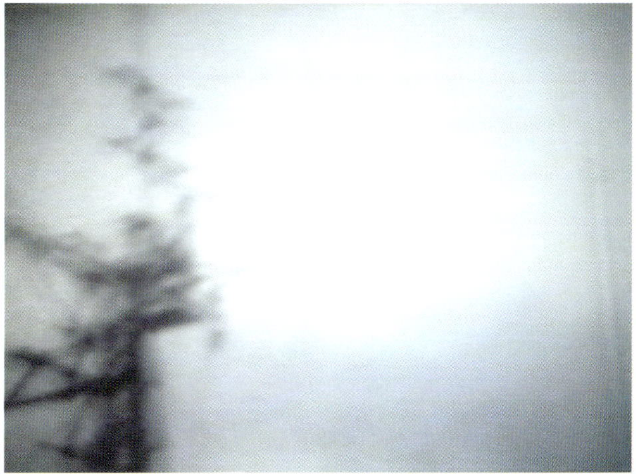

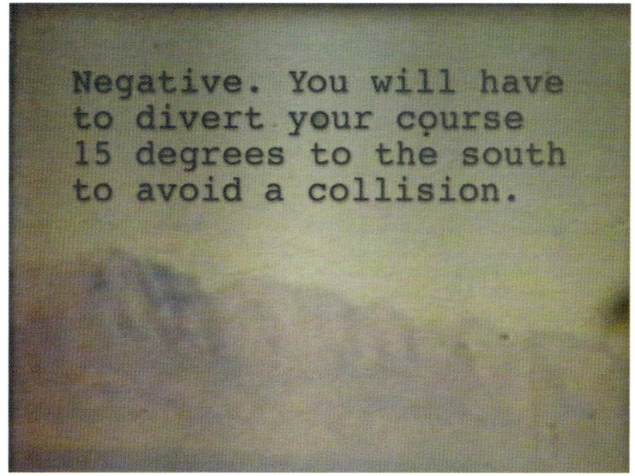
Negative. You will have
to divert your course
15 degrees to the south
to avoid a collision.

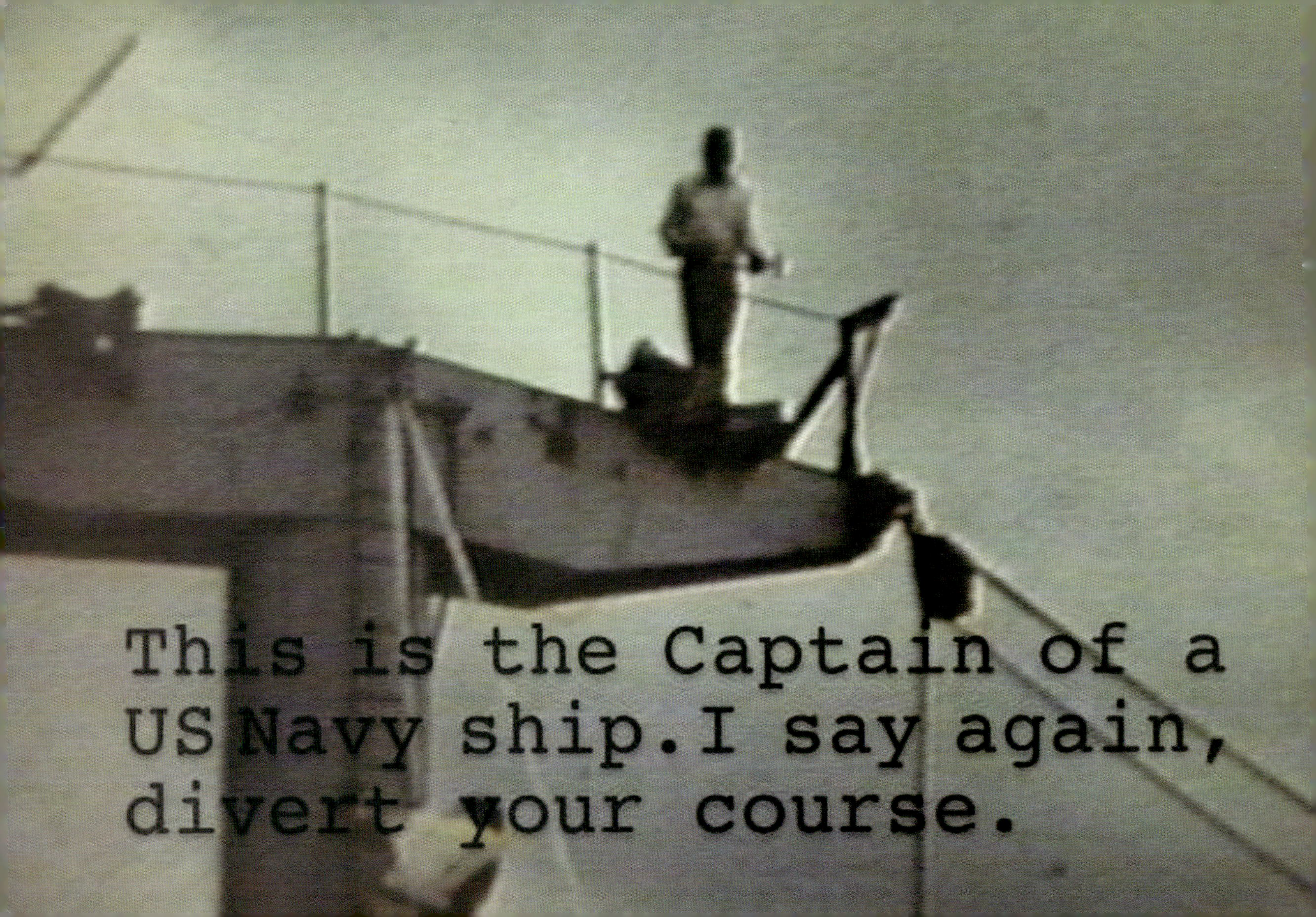
This is the Captain of a US Navy ship. I say again, divert your course.

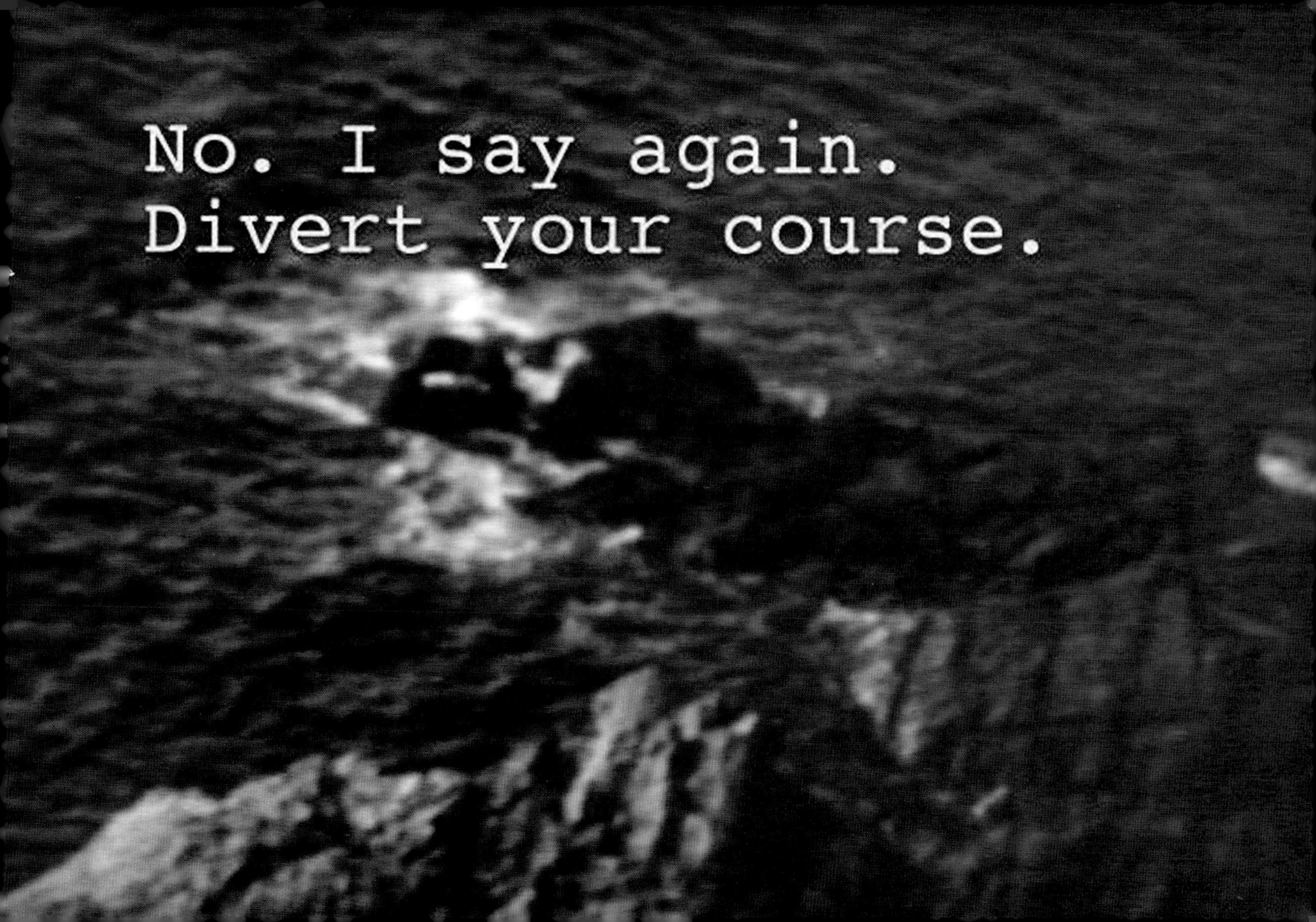
No. I say again.
Divert your course.

This is the USS Lincoln, the second largest ship in the US Atlantic fleet.

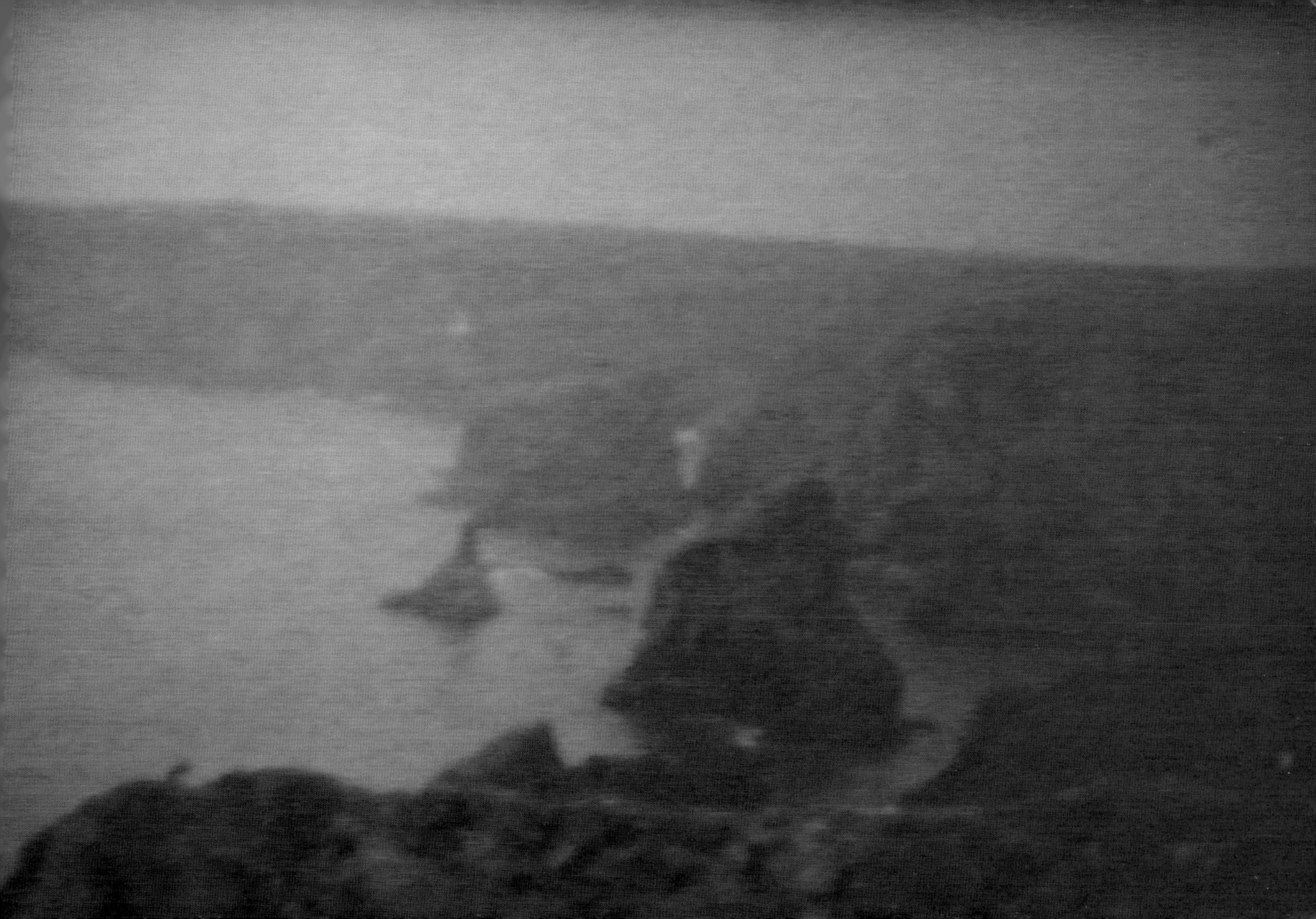

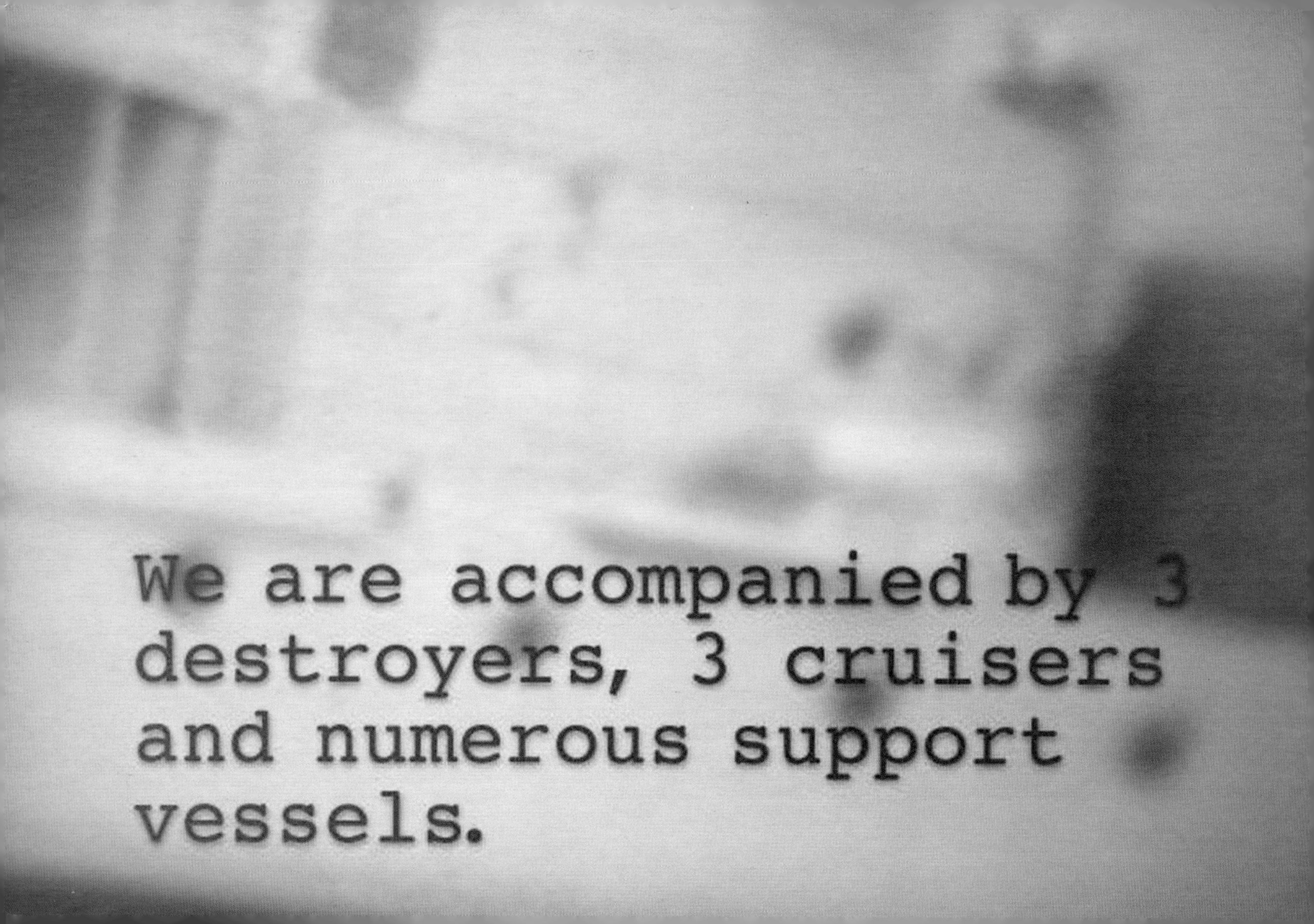
We are accompanied by 3
destroyers, 3 cruisers
and numerous support
vessels.

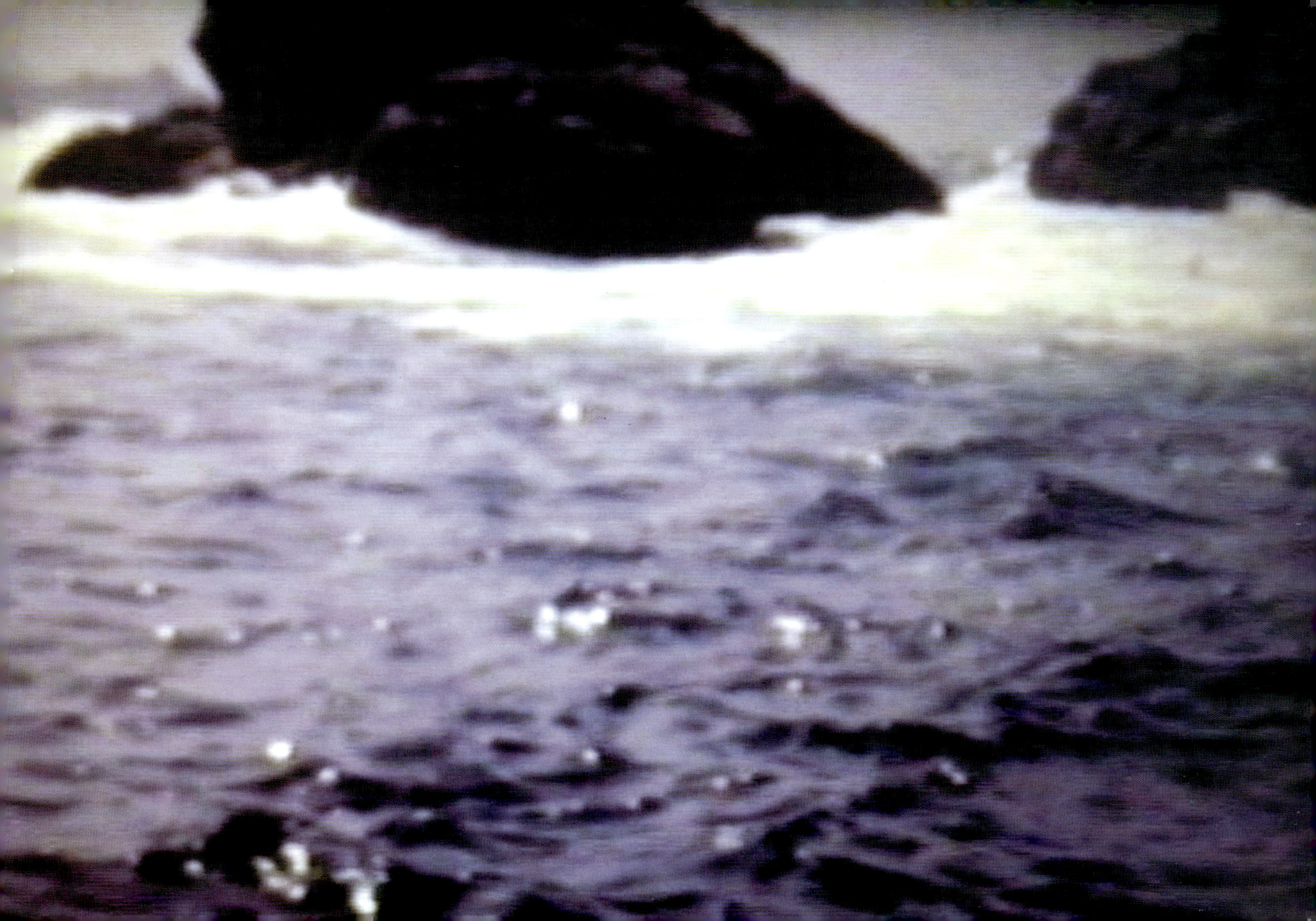

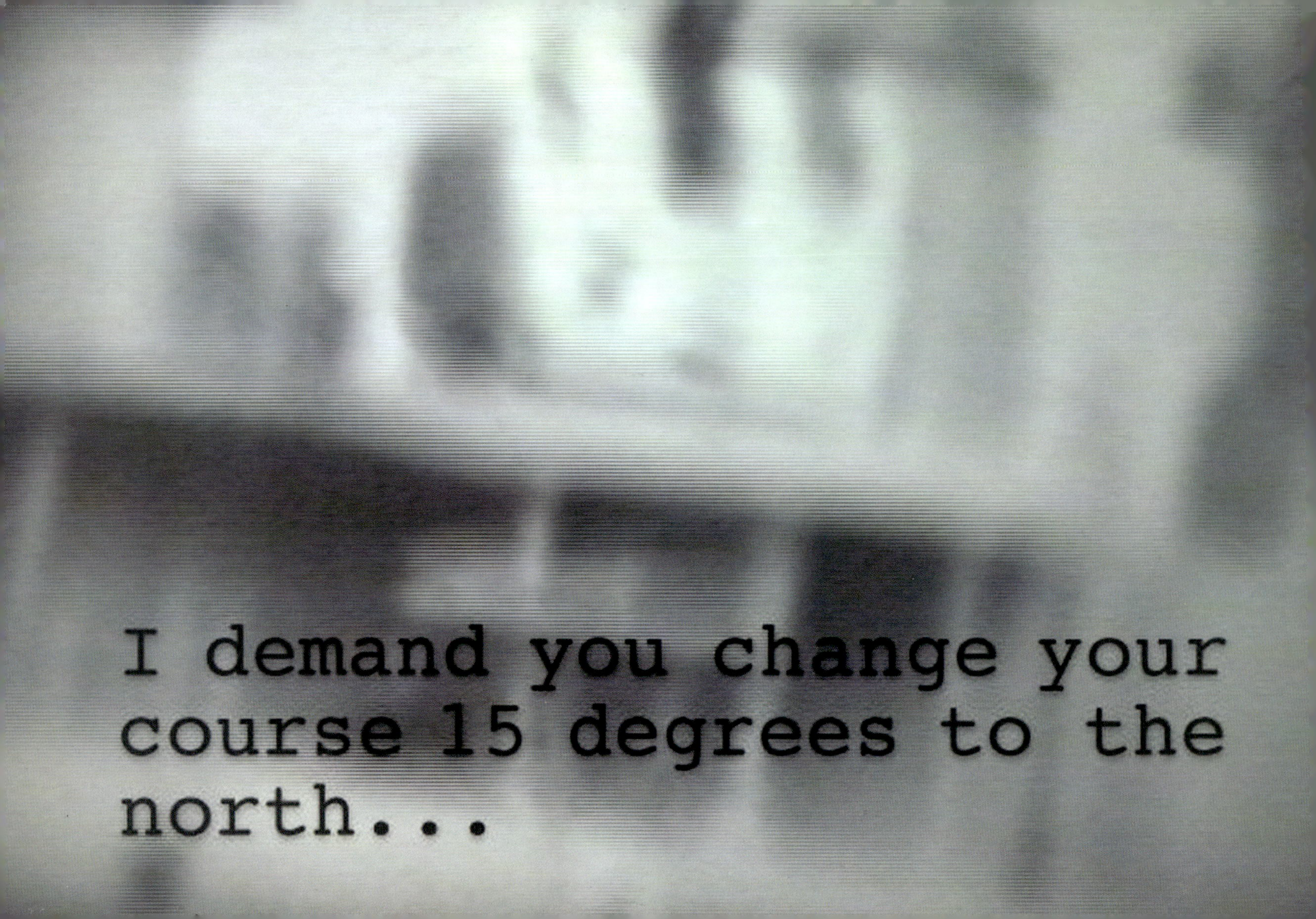
I demand you change your course 15 degrees to the north...

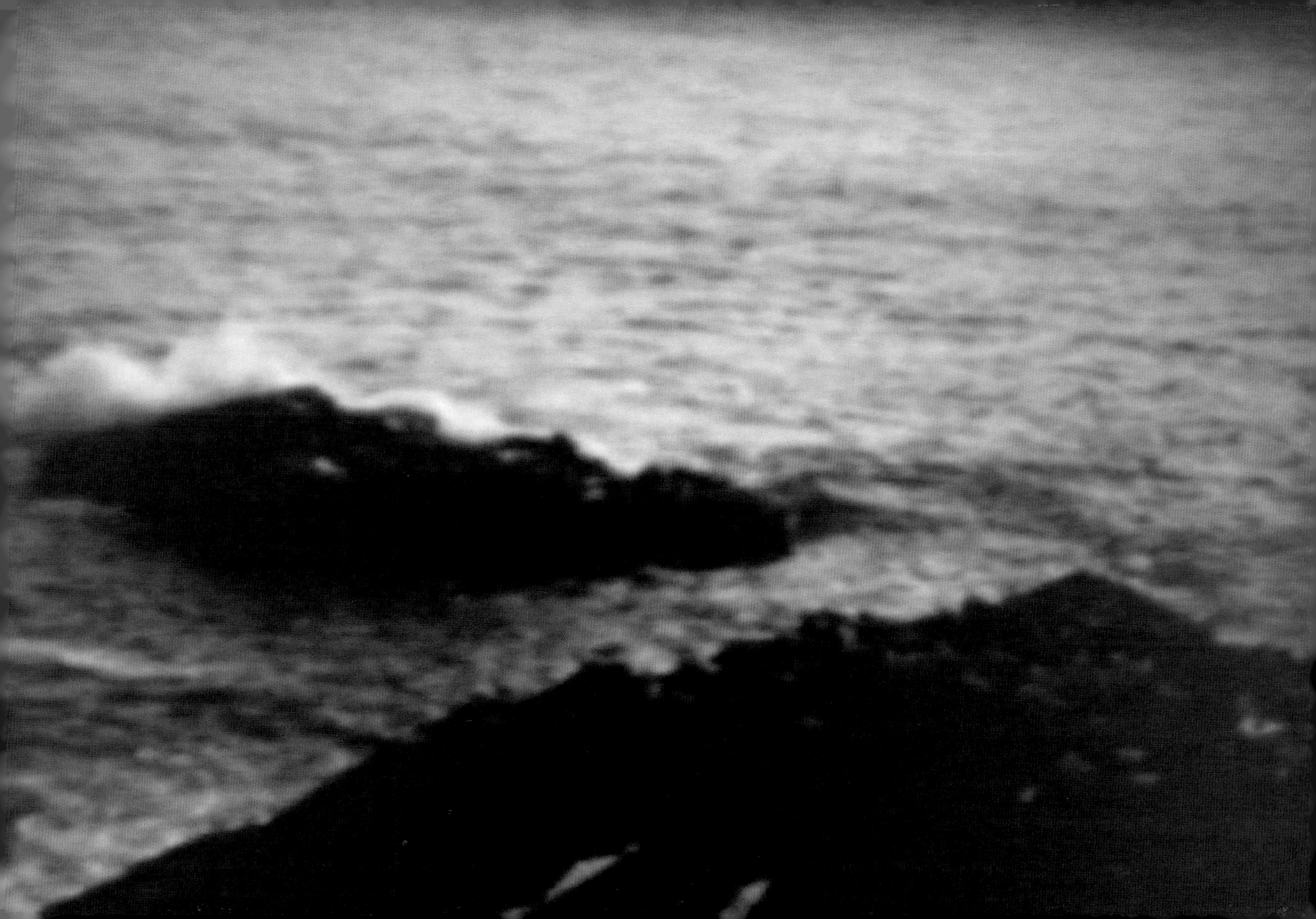

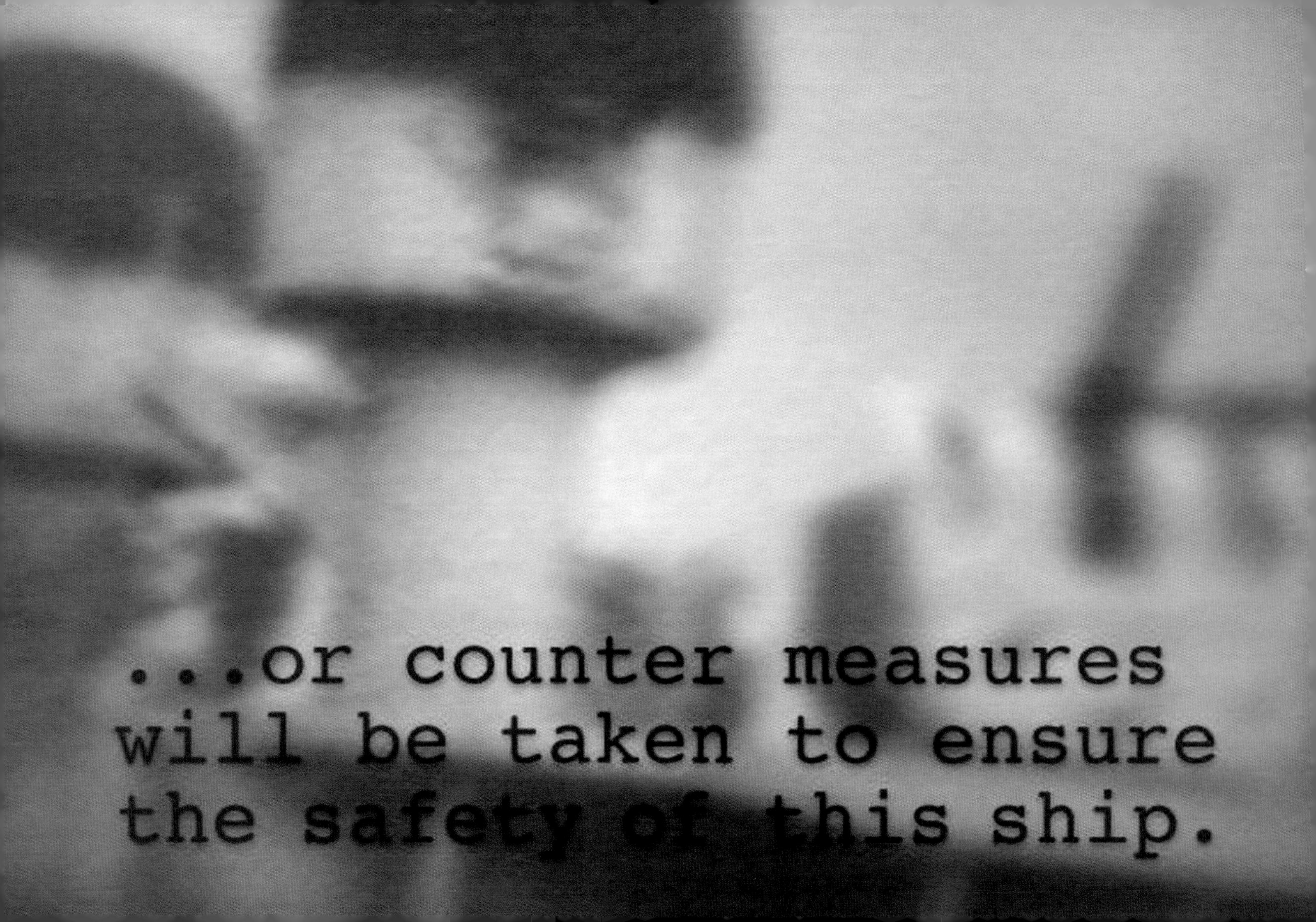
...or counter measures
will be taken to ensure
the safety of this ship.

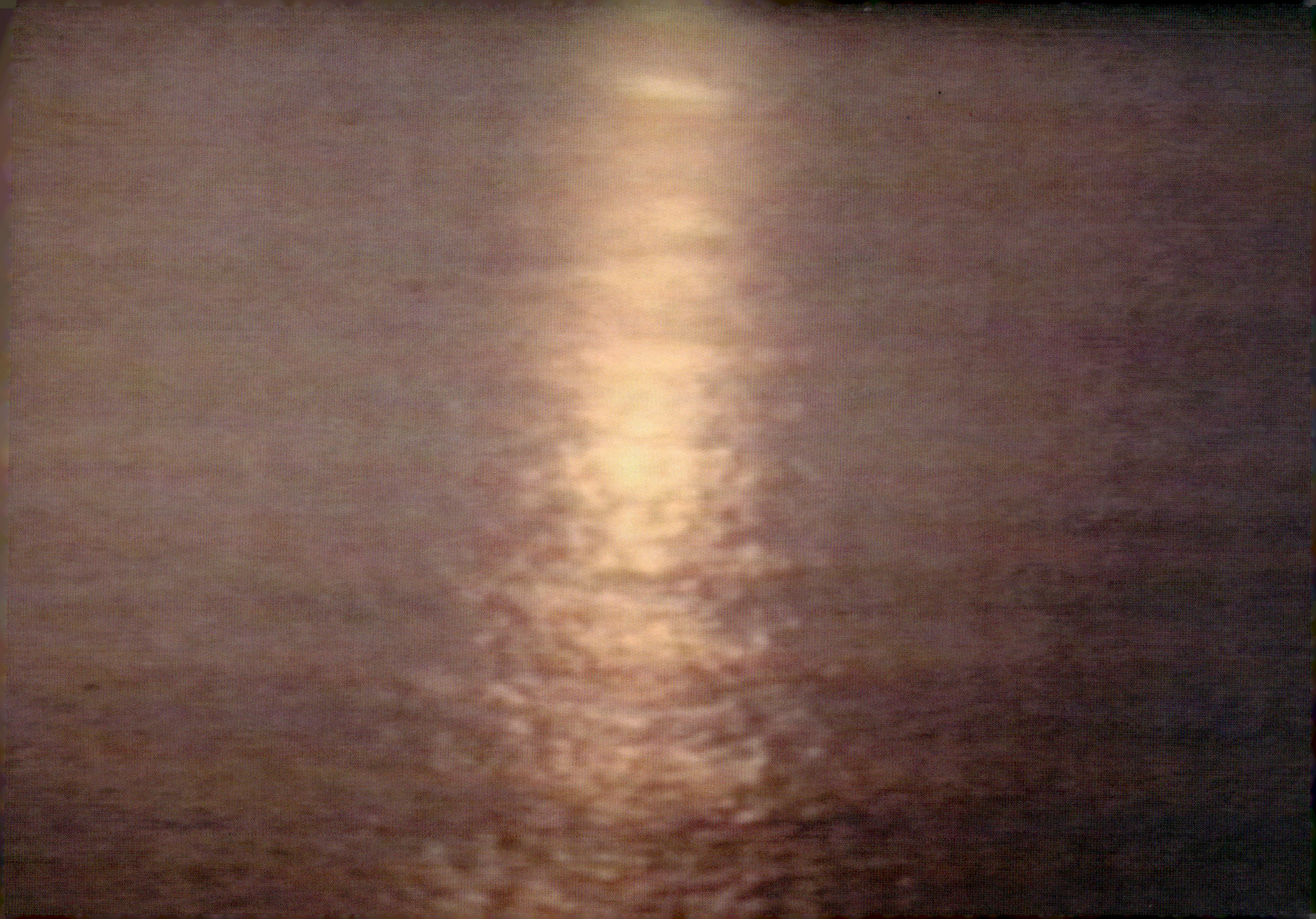

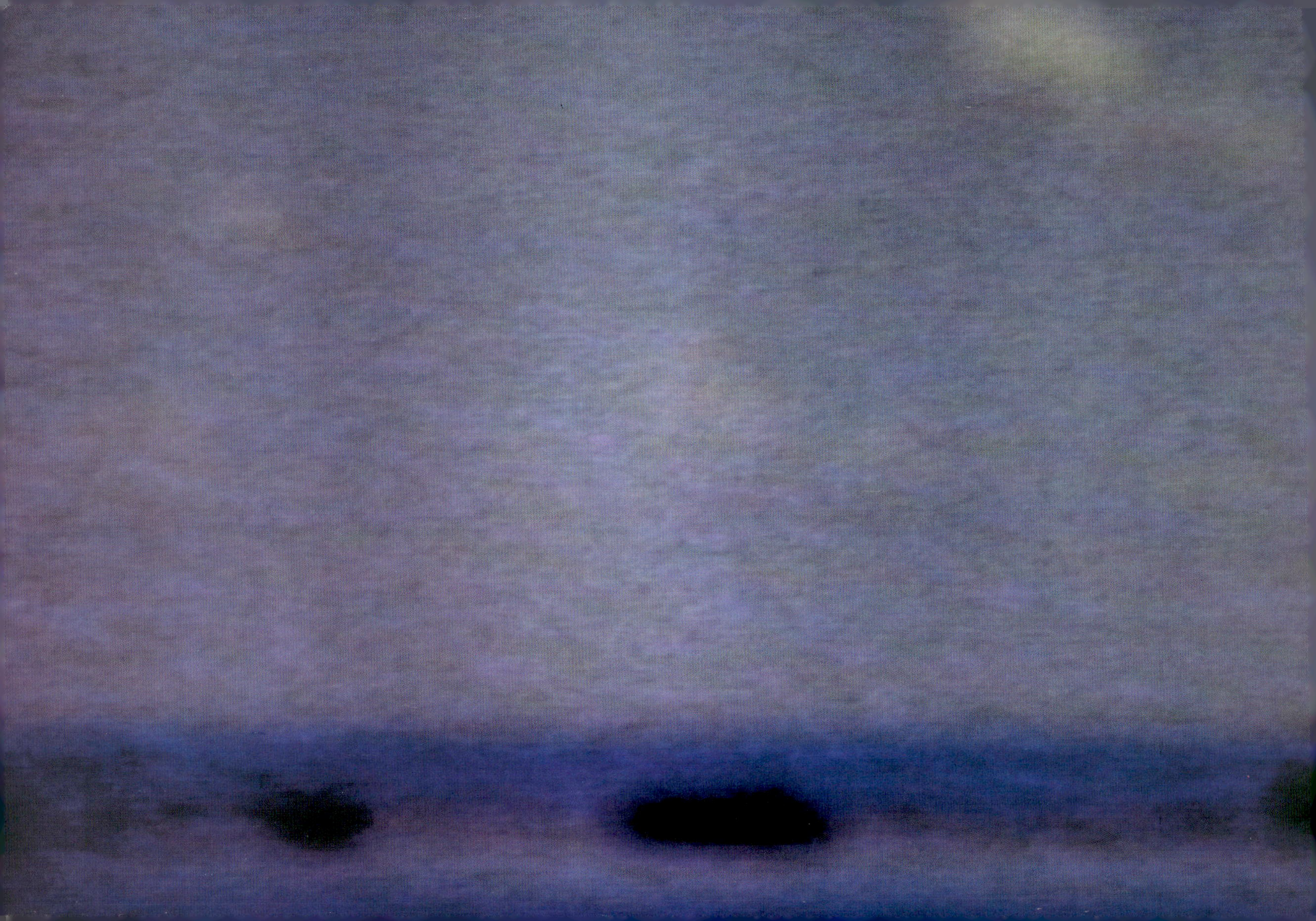

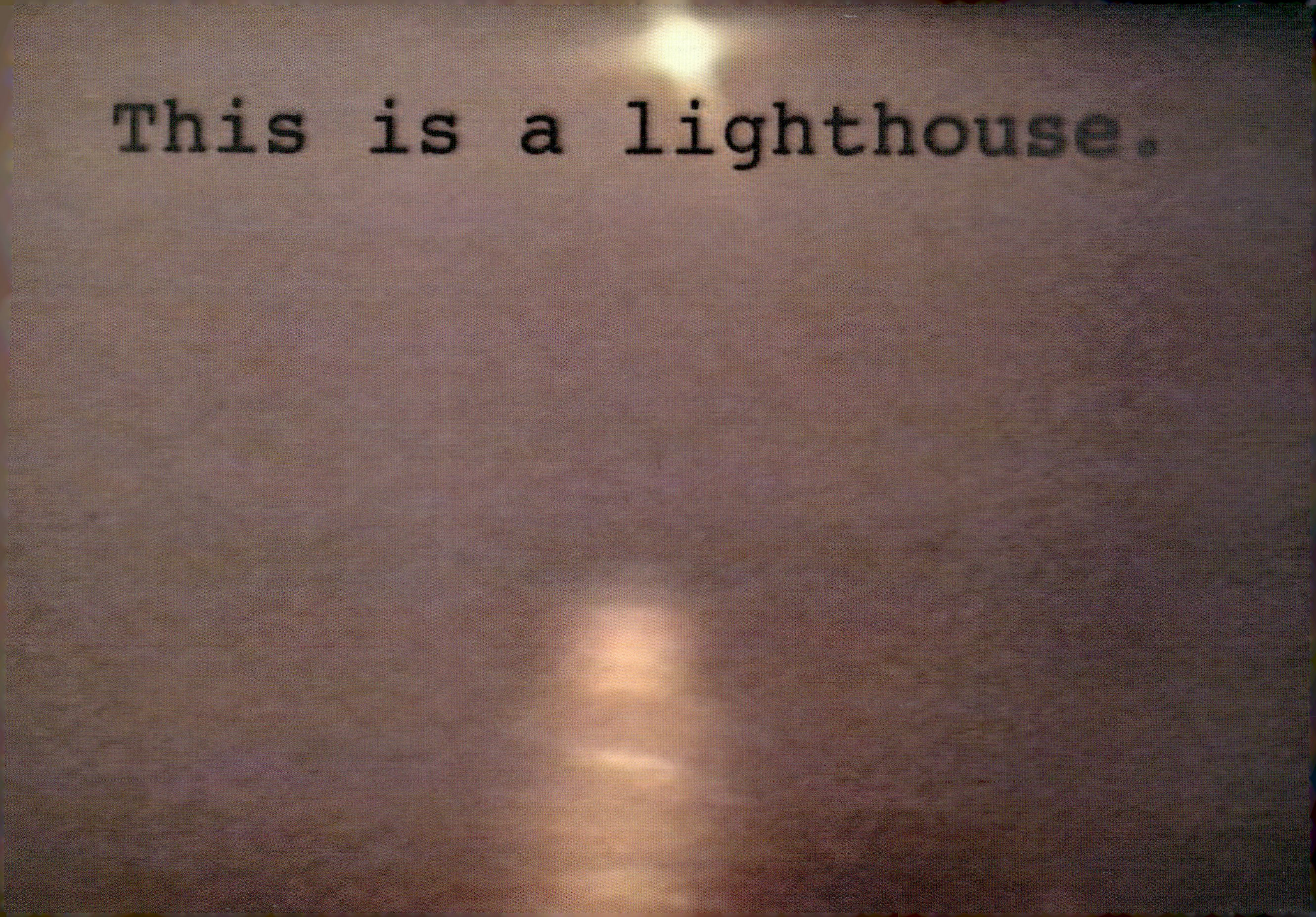
This is a lighthouse.

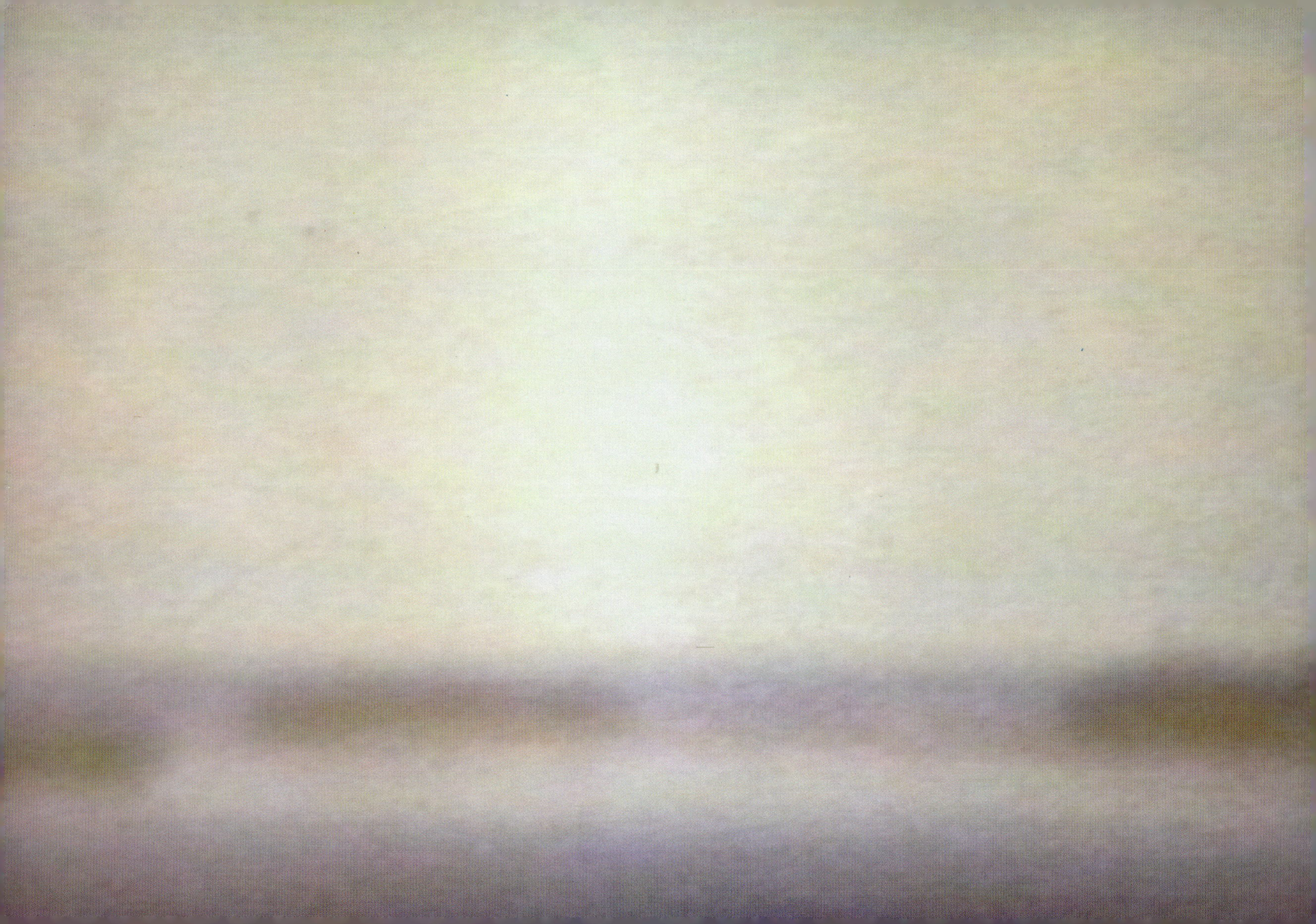

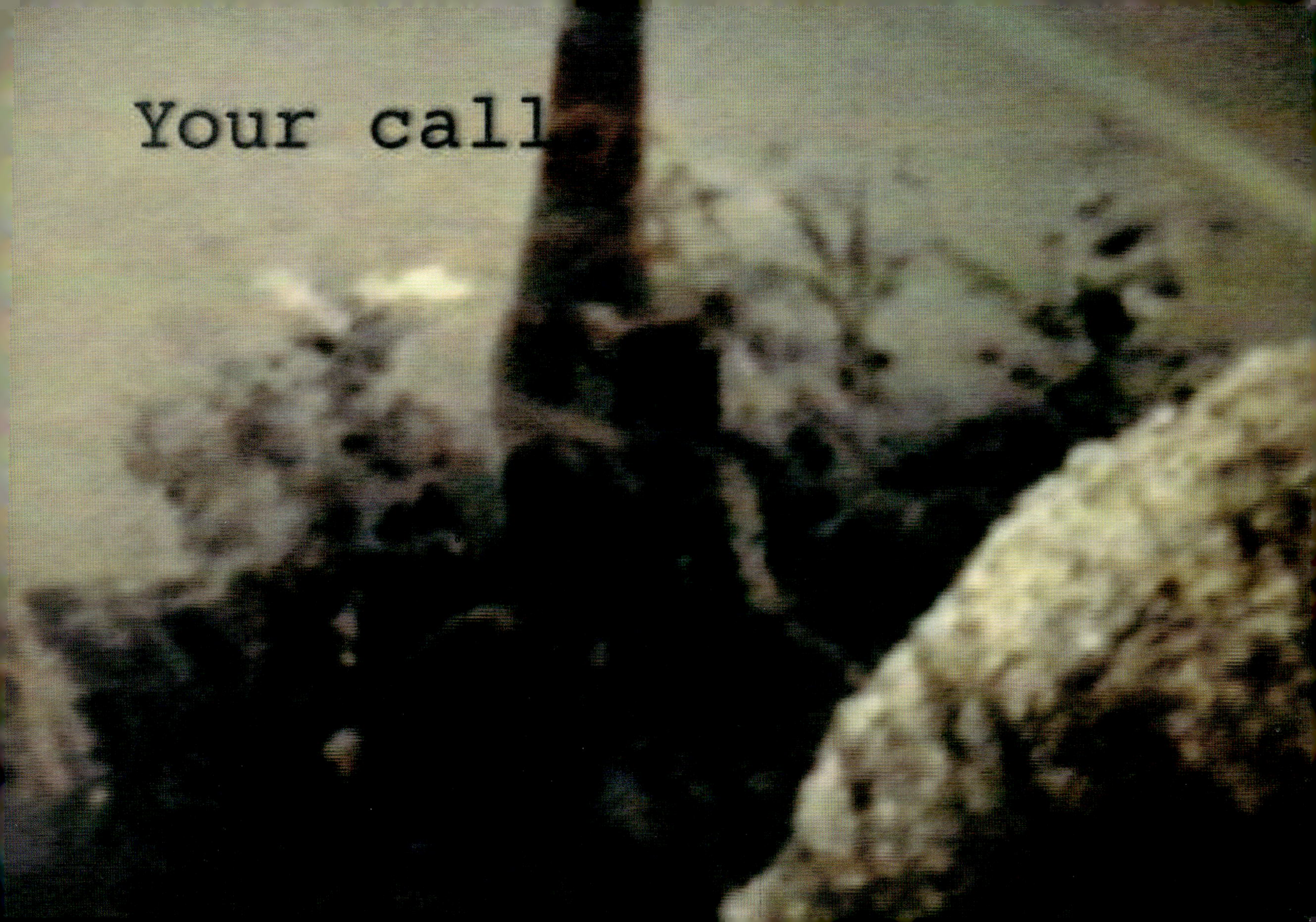
Your call

0398: Oregon

Matt's Gallery, 1999

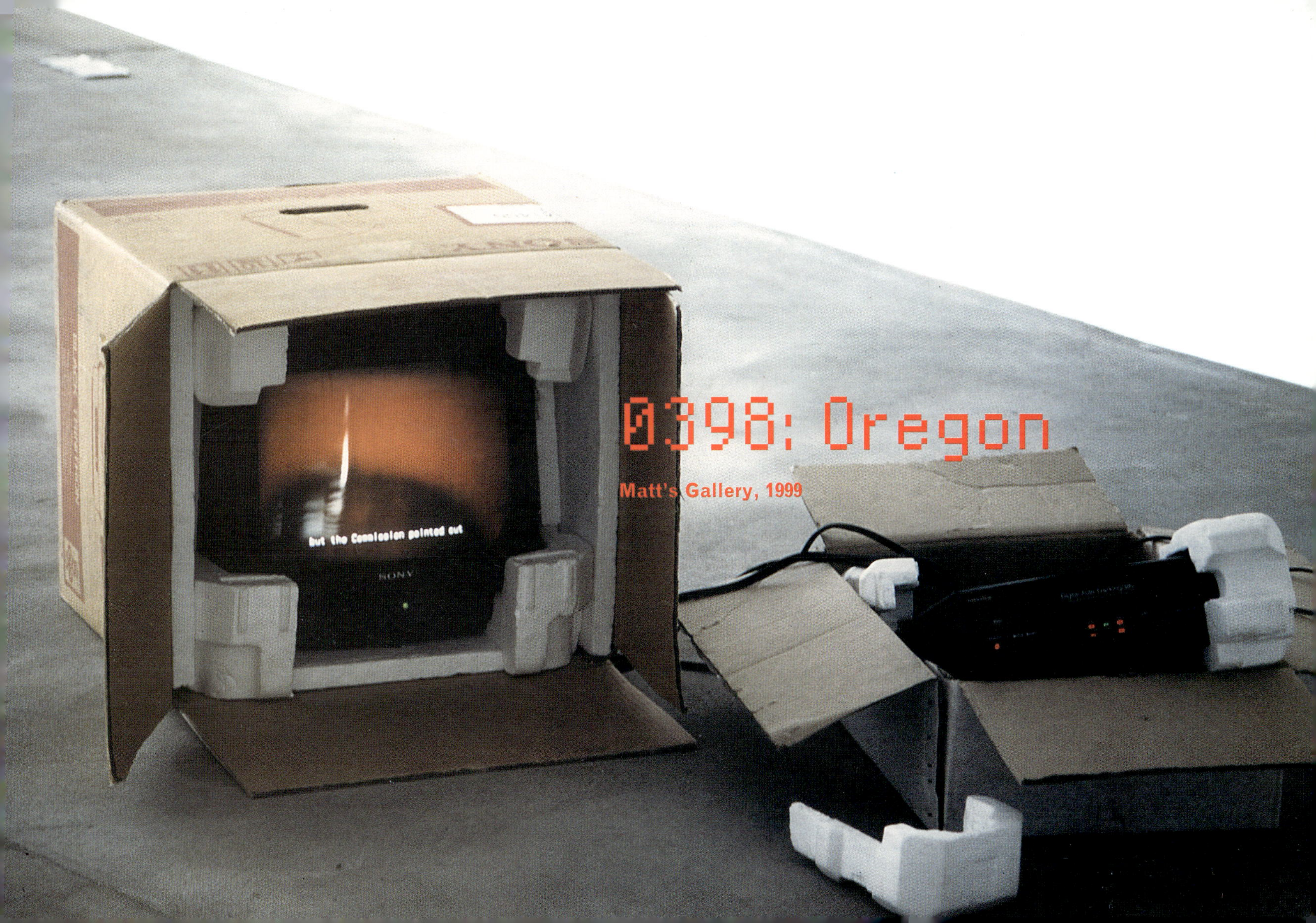

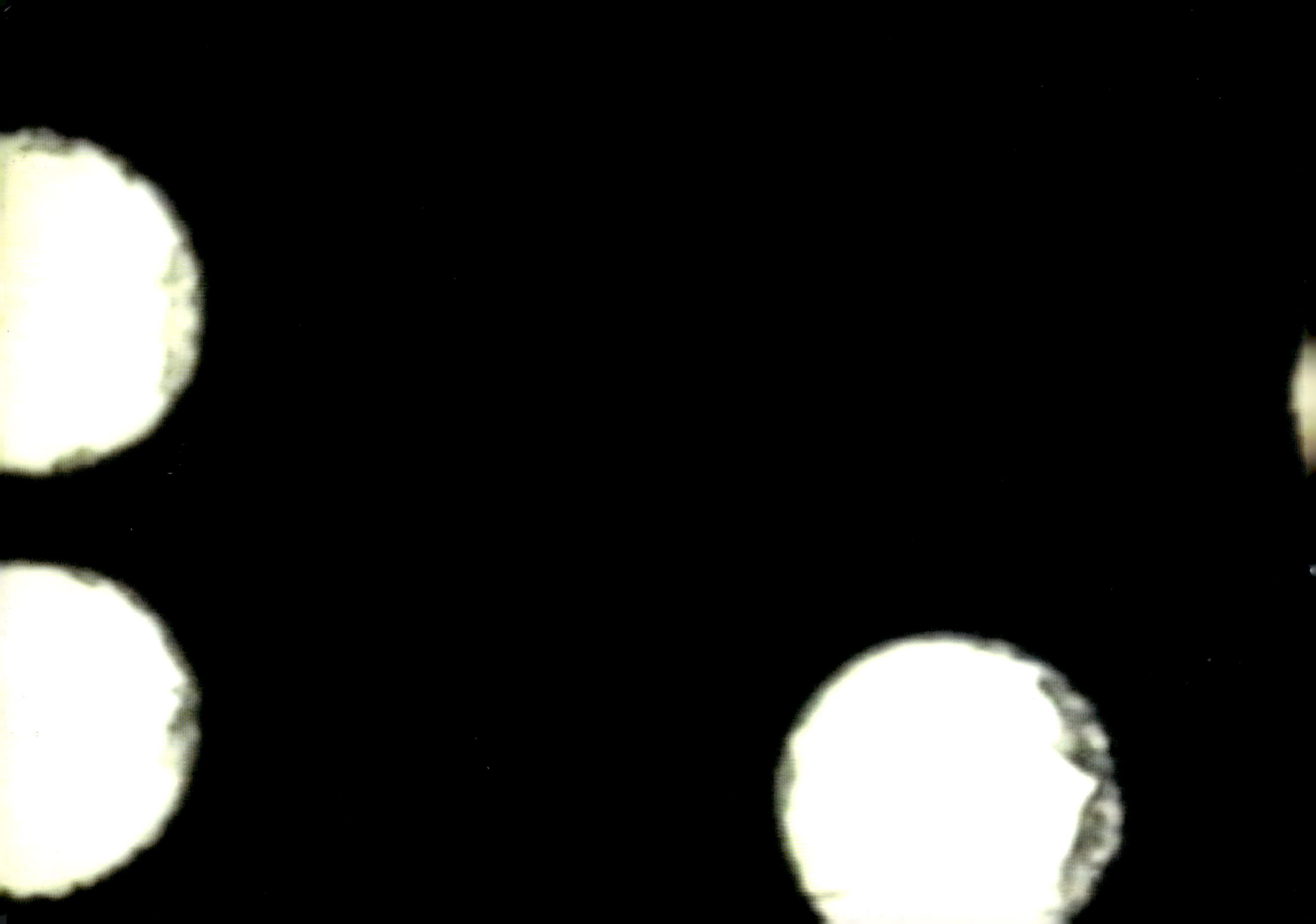

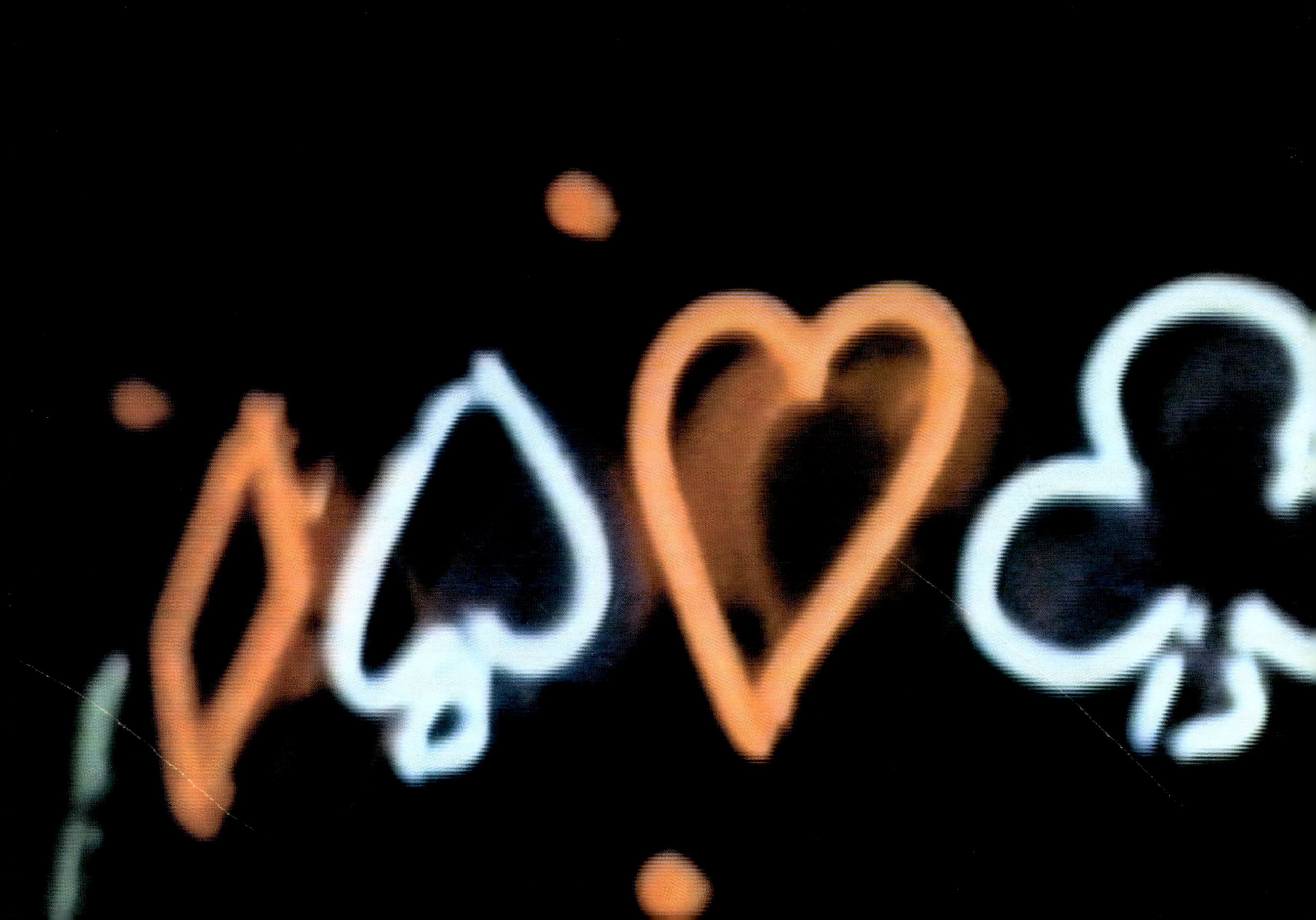

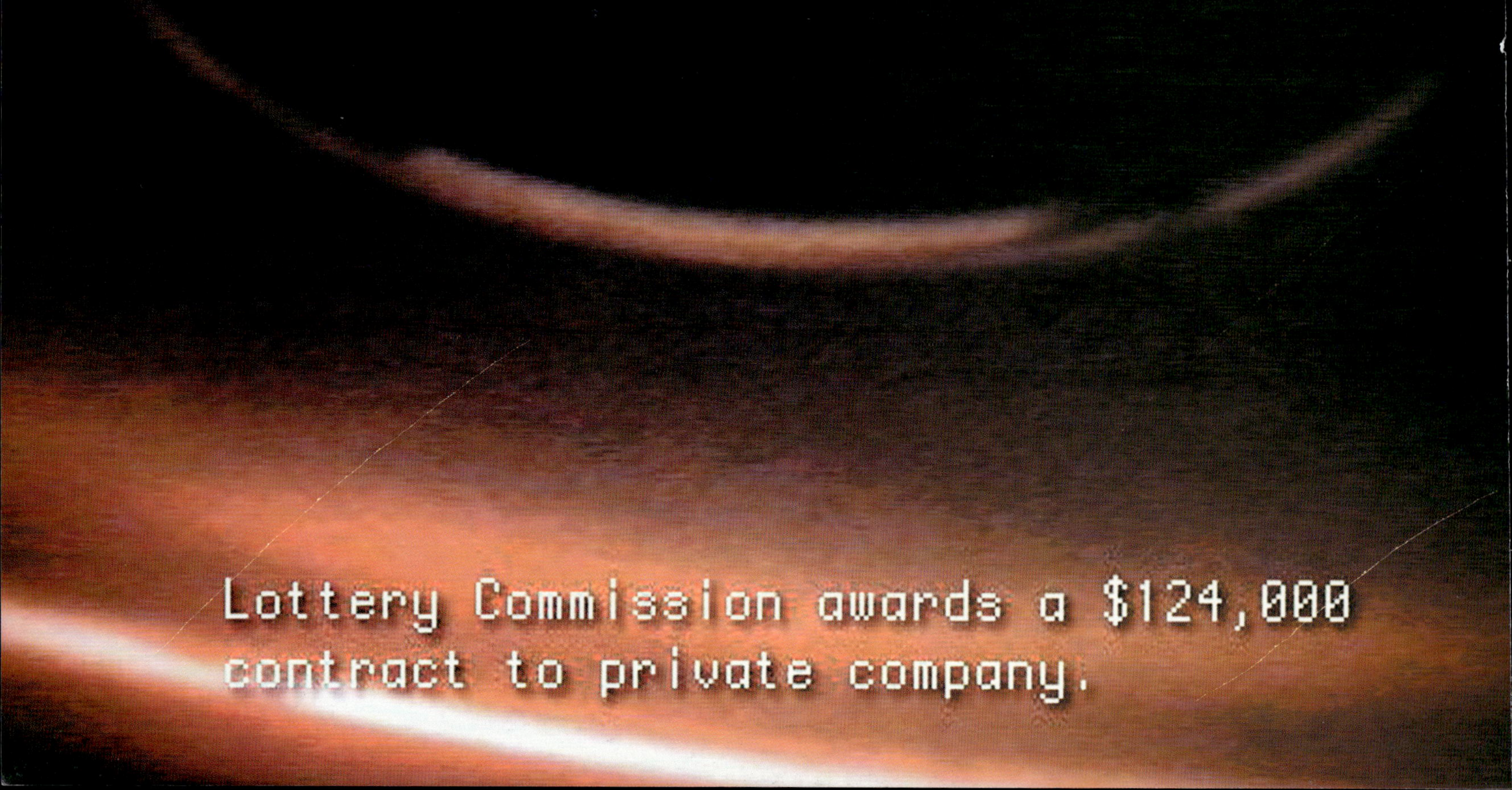
Lottery Commission awards a $124,000
contract to private company.

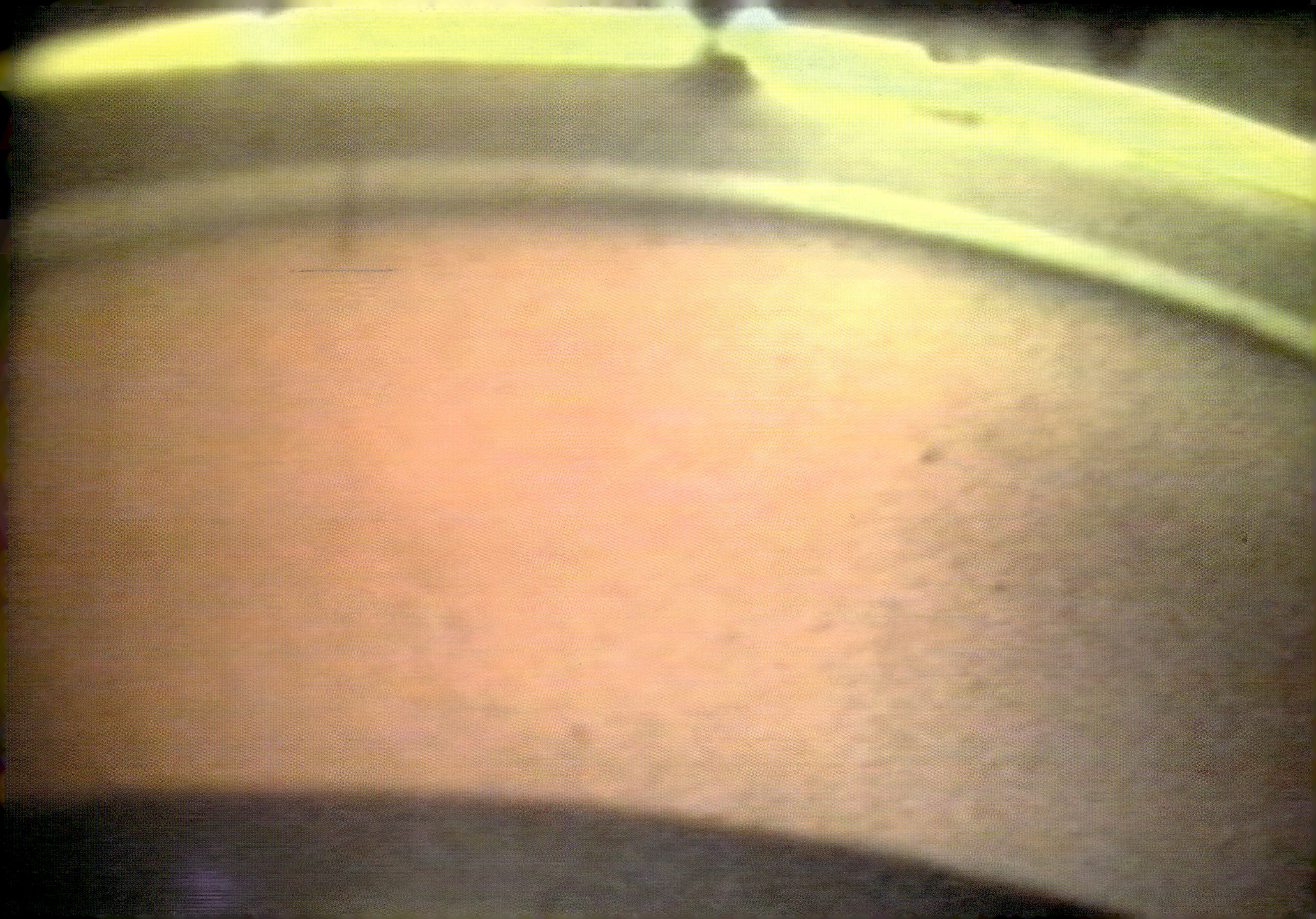

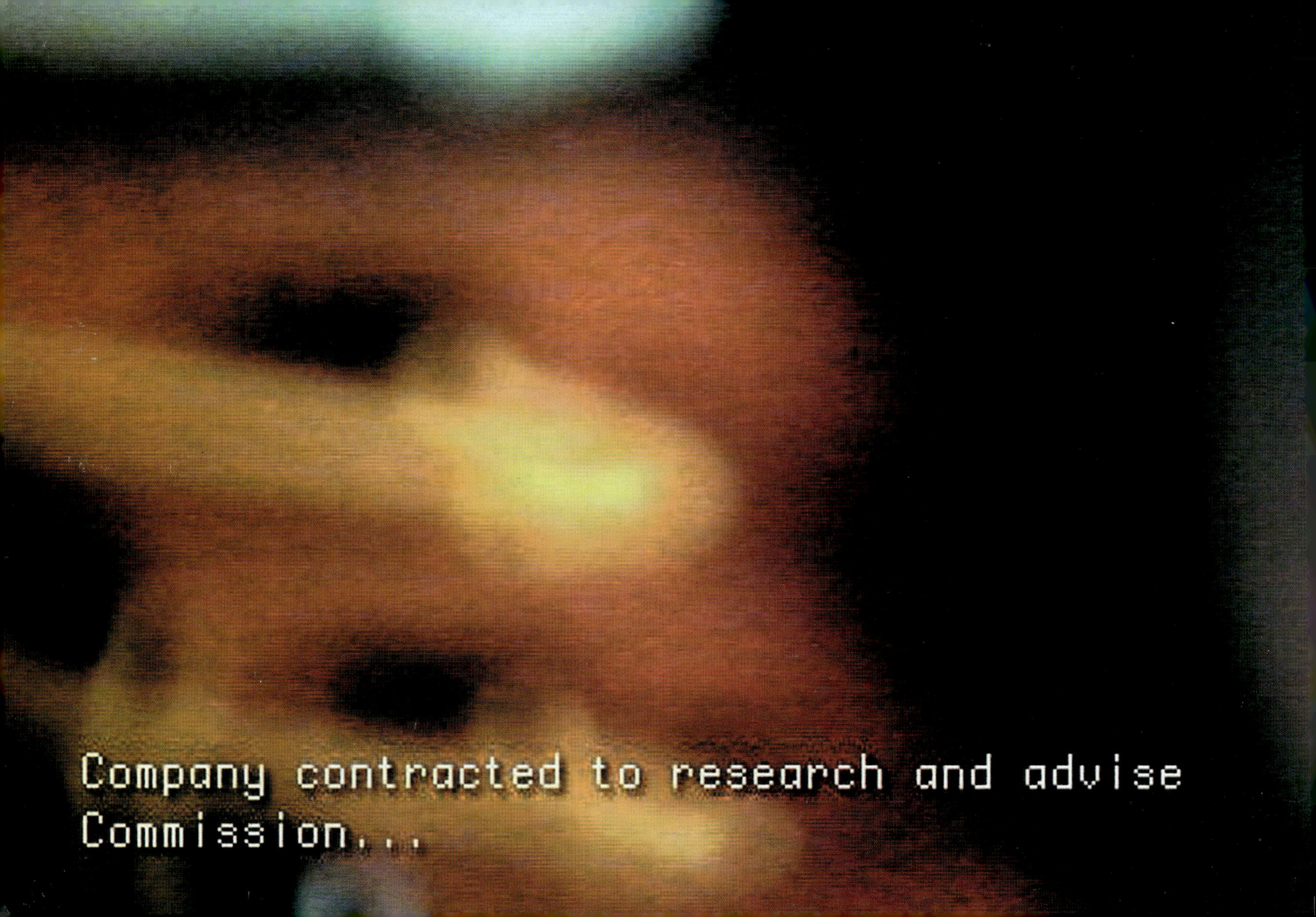
Company contracted to research and advise
Commission...

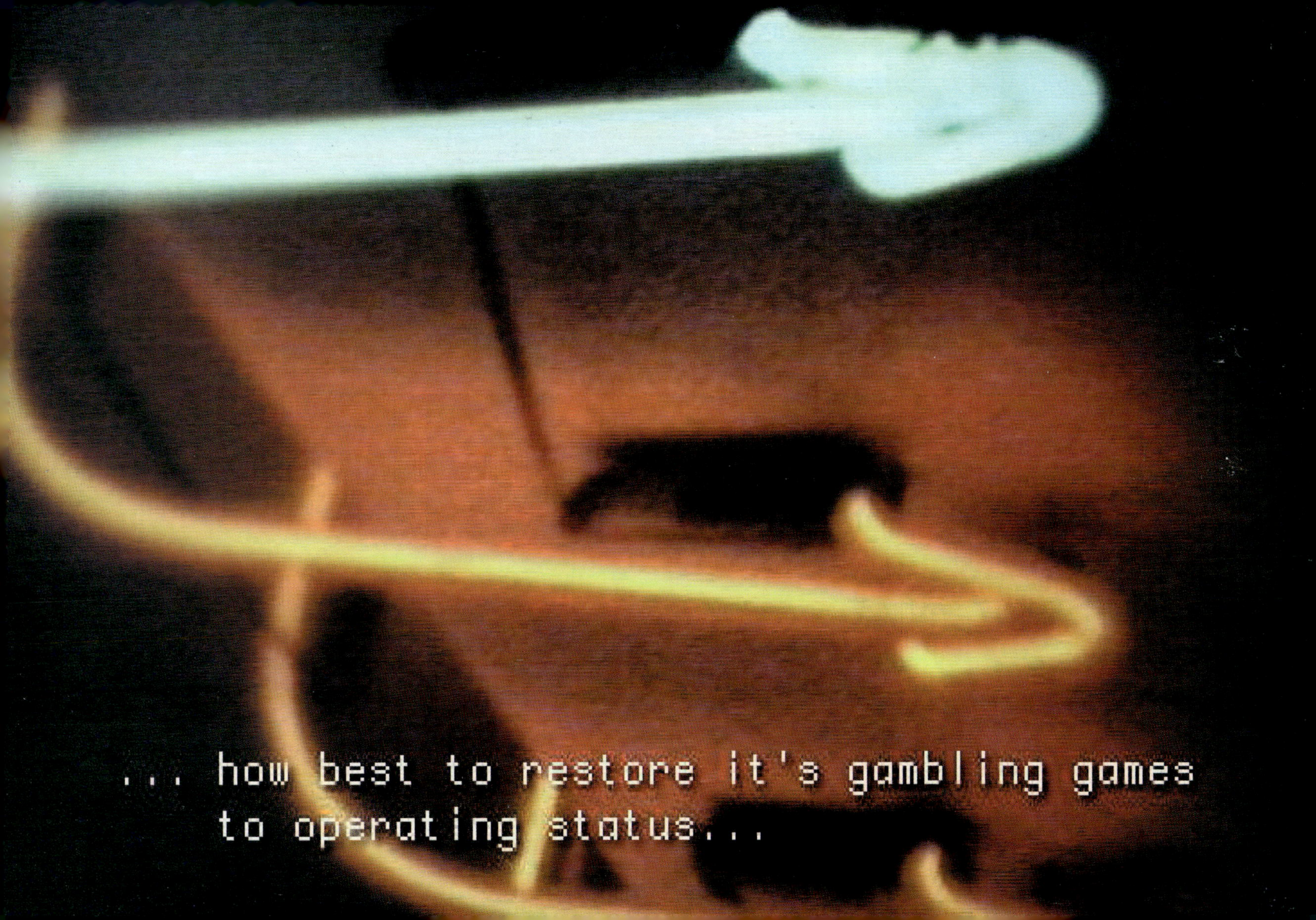
... how best to restore it's gambling games
to operating status...

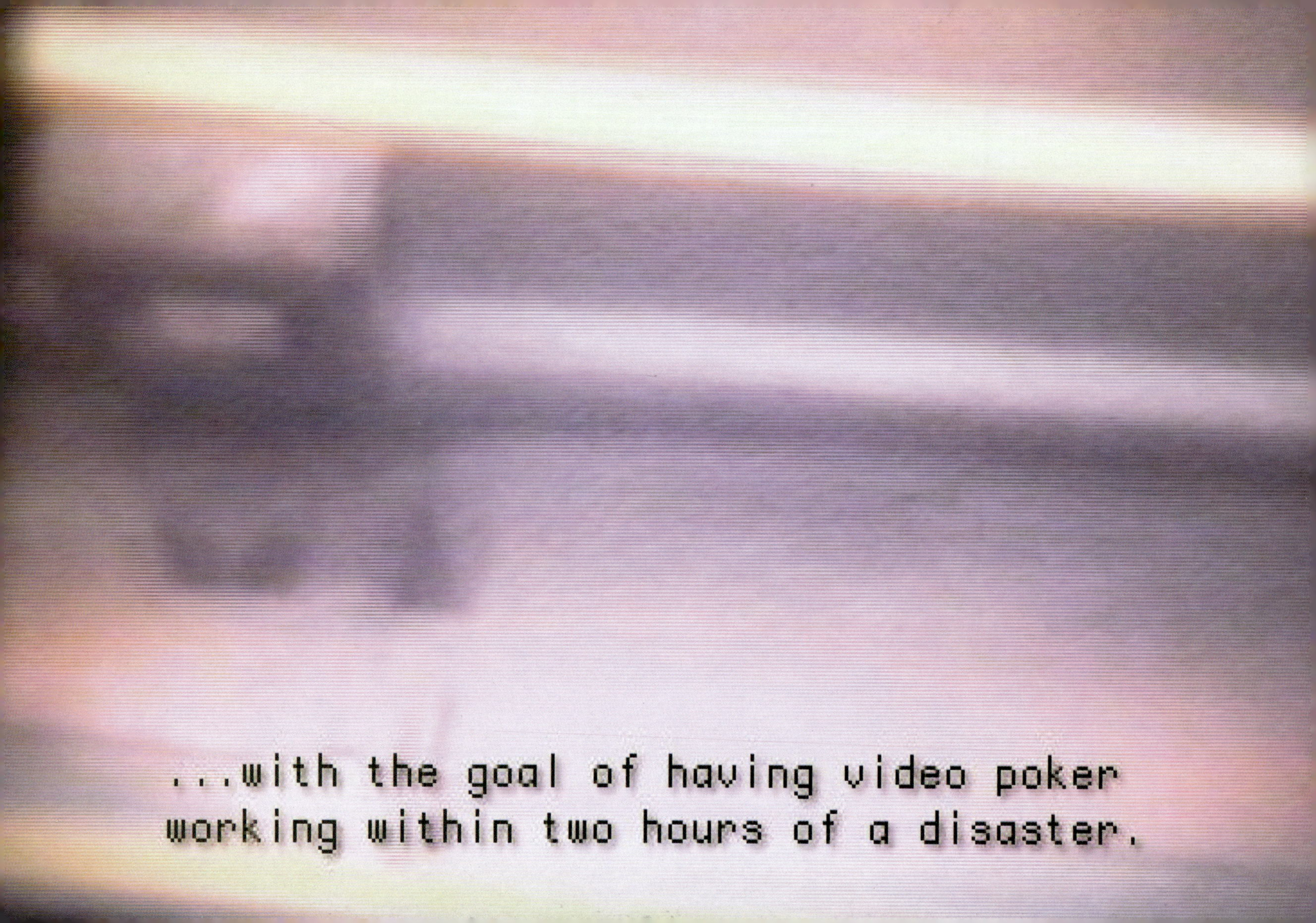
...with the goal of having video poker
working within two hours of a disaster.

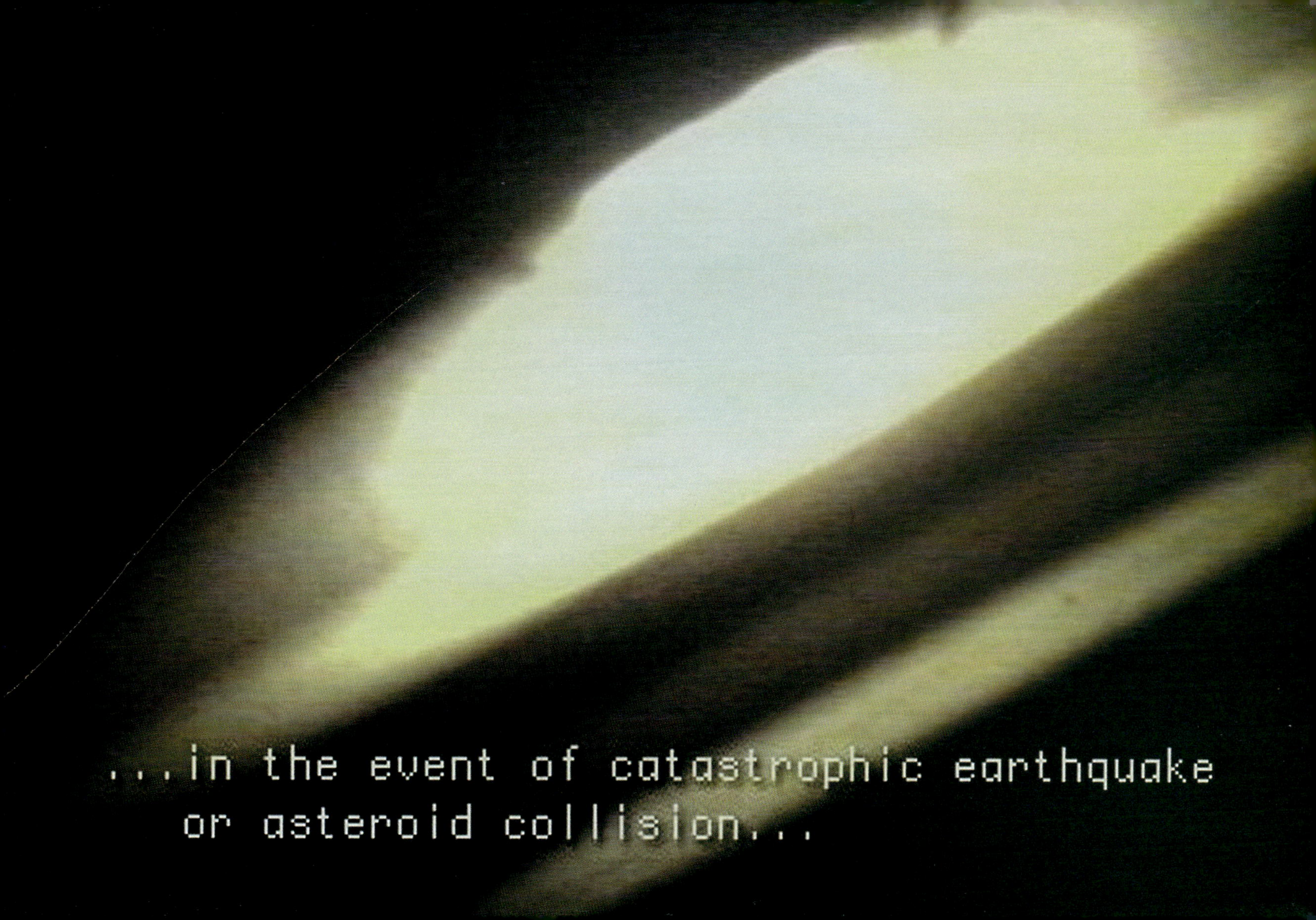
...in the event of catastrophic earthquake
or asteroid collision...

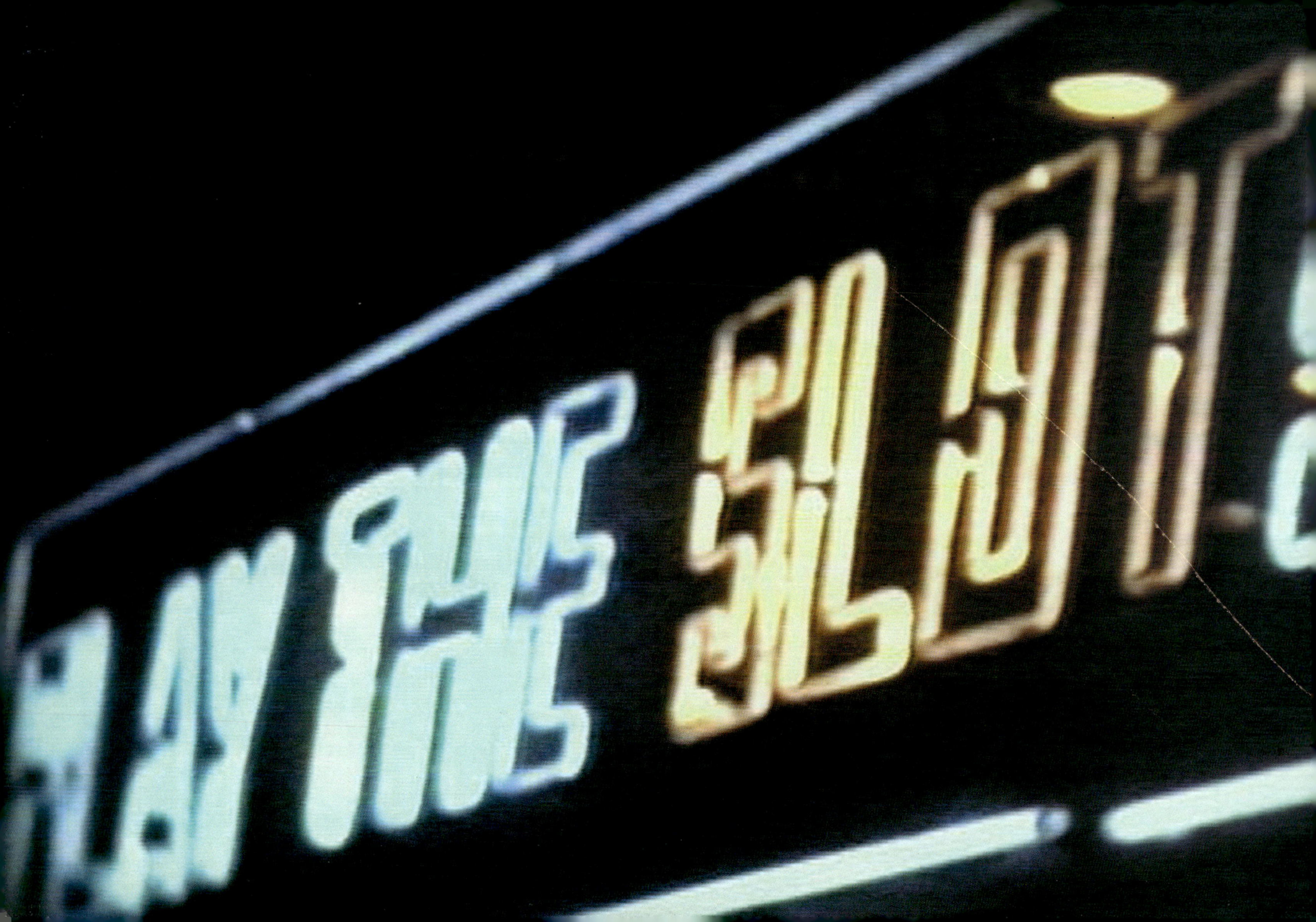

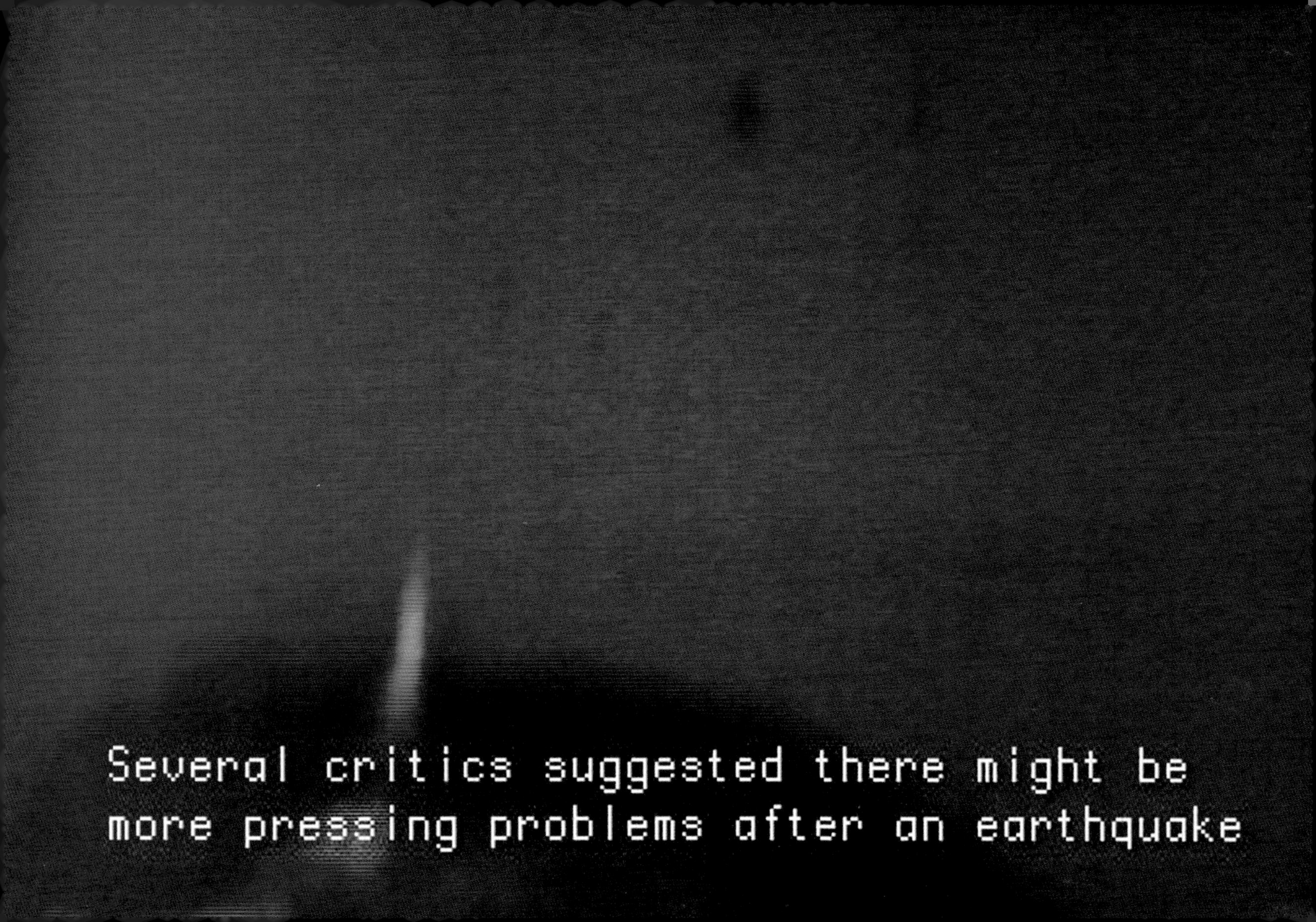
Several critics suggested there might be
more pressing problems after an earthquake

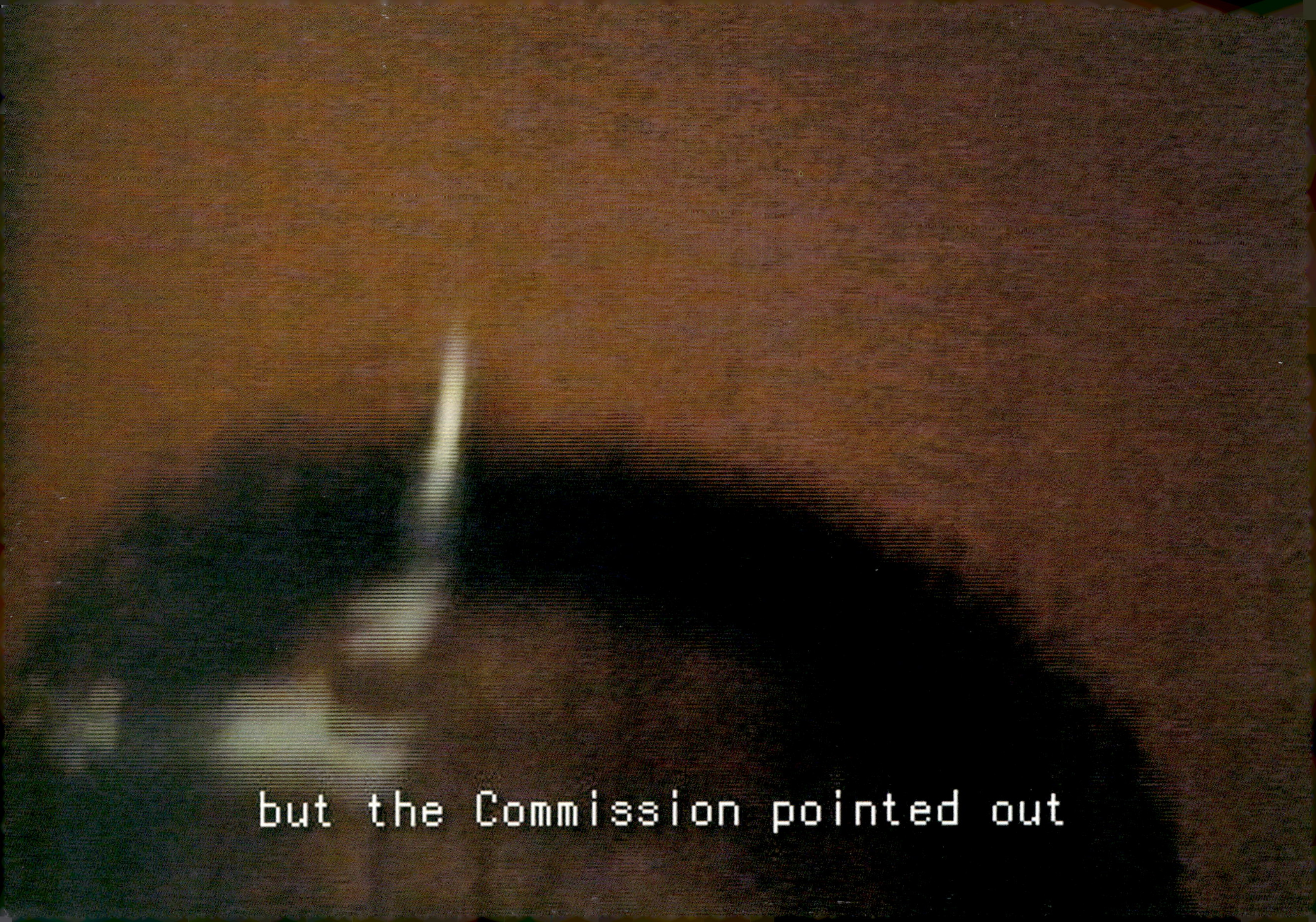
but the Commission pointed out

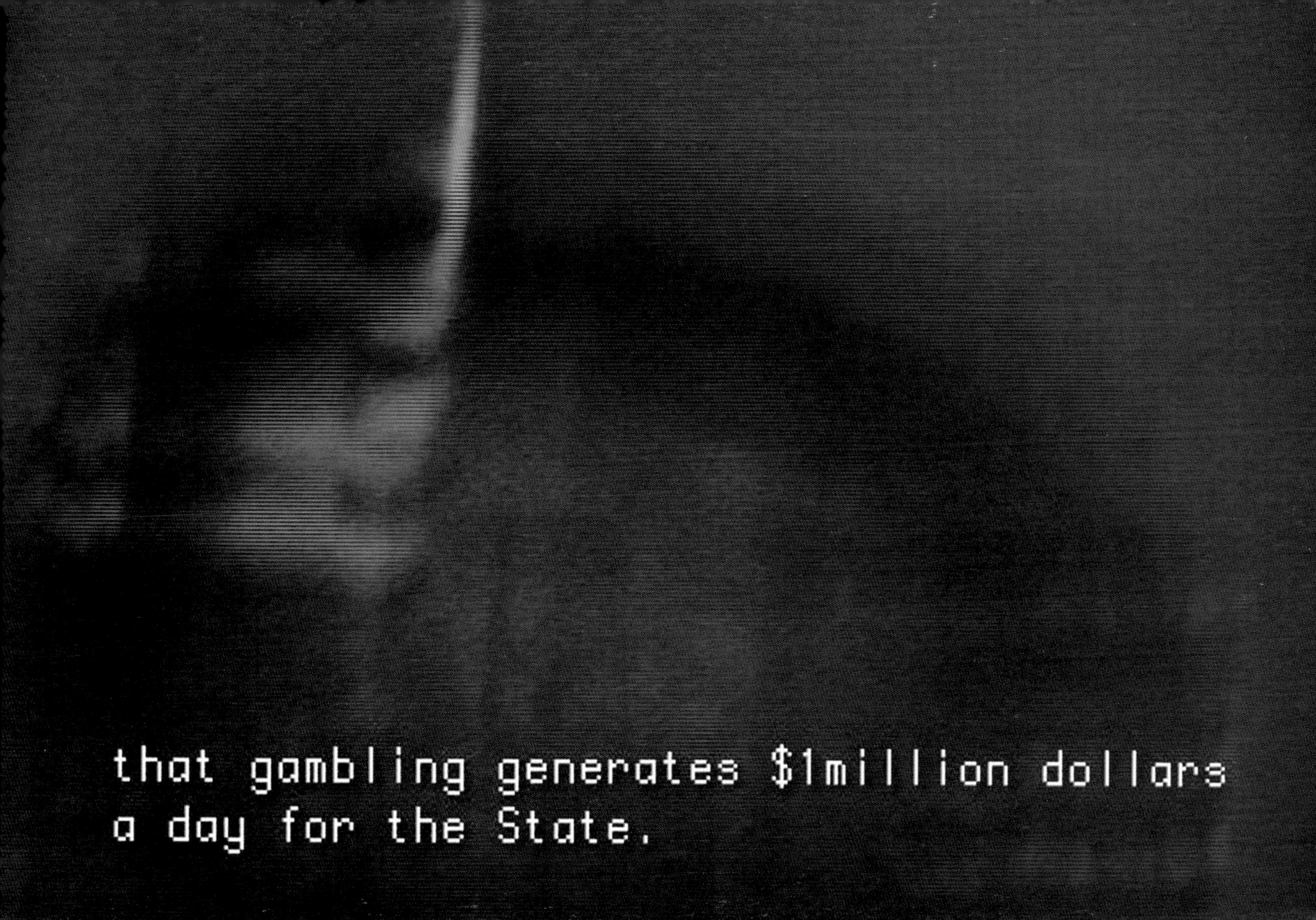
that gambling generates $1million dollars
a day for the State.

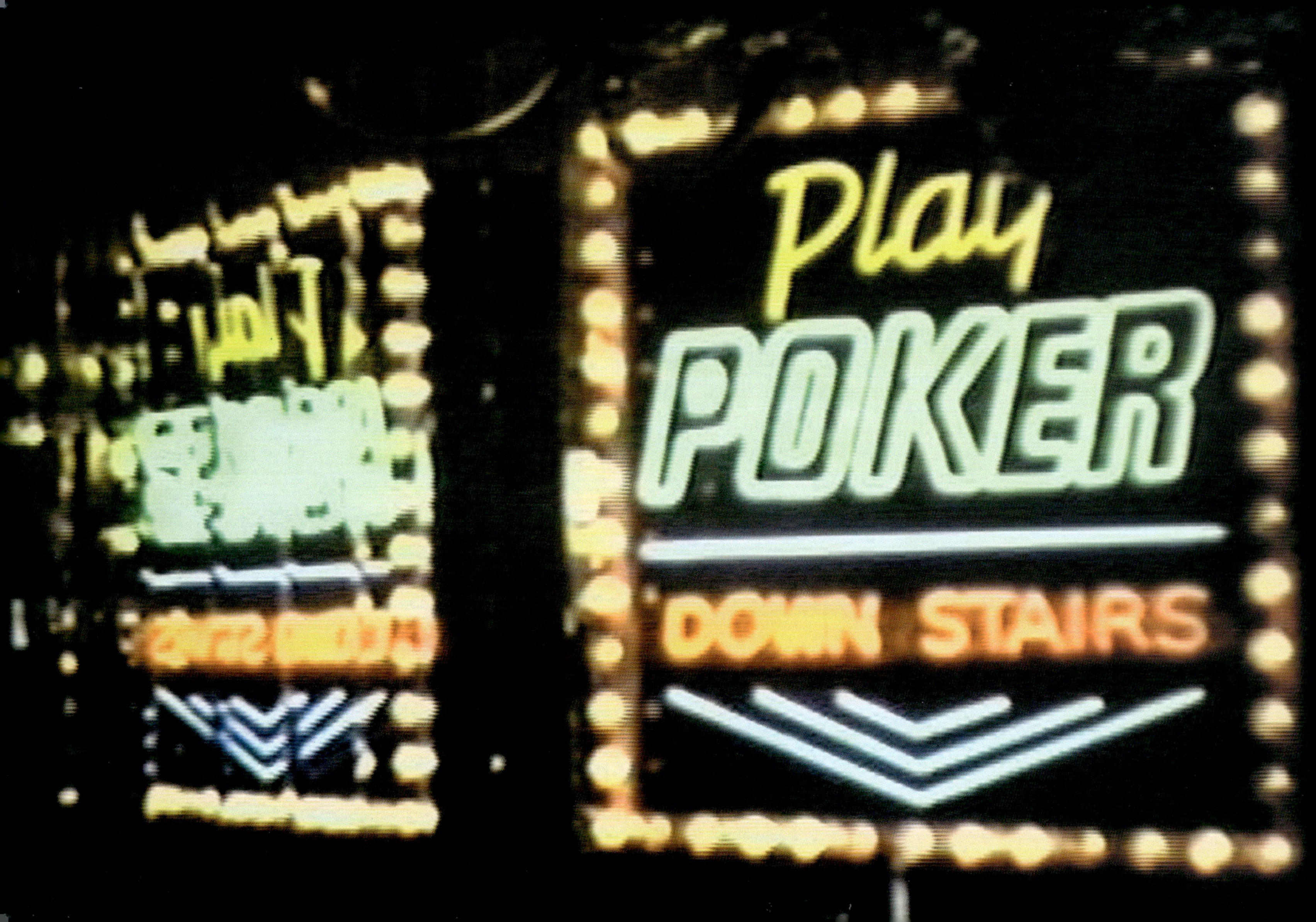
Play
POKER
DOWN STAIRS

Ian Hunt

Lost Horizons

There are places you get to visit and there are those that, while you know they exist, remain unvisited and therefore fabulous. You may hear someone's account of their voyage, hold anchors for it in the form of photos, documents or souvenirs, but still fail to integrate the fascination of their story and of strongly realised details within a whole picture, or within the set of assumptions you carry in your head. Such moments of fascination are capable of disorganizing sensations, thoughts and understandings (part of the definition of the sublime); they cause you to erect a whole set of hypotheses, guesses and explanations, or simply to project in imagination spaces that are real enough but which you have never before had reason to think of. Afterwards you may be able to piece together the story in the framework of what you know, or can find out. There are actually rather few things that are experienced as anomalies that cannot finally be explained. But the explanation may not be enough to exhaust the initial fascination, whether it is the result of first hand experience or that proxy experience that possesses its own vivid reality, when you form pictures on the basis of a verbal explanation that cannot be dislodged. When I read in Melanie Jackson's enviably quick prose about the grain destined for Saudi racehorses in Cardiff dock, dyed pink to distinguish it from grain for human consumption, the surprise of the detail – the part you could not make up – made vividly material and visible that largely unseen trade in bulk commodities that is still conveyed across the seas. There are things you only find out if you go there.

I know a man who spent over a decade researching the history of Antarctic exploration. His book, a cultural history of the sentiments of those drawn to explore the poles, was published and was widely praised. And then (on a commission from *Condé Naste Traveller* magazine), he went there. He sailed on board a Russian icebreaker now fitted out for luxury cruises; visited the landscape that on paper he knew so well. Amongst the things he knew in advance was that many uncertainties of scale are discovered in the Antarctic landscape, so lacking in any reference points. But something he said after the trip still, as I think about it, frightens and amazes me. Travelling in a helicopter over a distant, frozen valley, features appeared that seemed to be of vast size. Snow was blown about below the helicopter which was now preparing to land amongst these same cliffs that were revealed to be far smaller than they had seemed from above. In the approach to touchdown he had mentally to collapse the imagined descent that remained to be travelled, so that each second of travel had to represent the equivalent of a great drop in altitude. Even so, his brain could not quite adjust to the revealed size of the isolated valley; the feeling persisted that, though impressive was in fact a model of a far larger landscape that he had only just witnessed from above, which was still perhaps contained within this substantial but smaller replica. His account magnifies something that any air traveller has noticed: that there is a radical lack of fit between views from above and from those on the ground, which cannot be comprehended even by devoted attention to all the moments of a descent. There is no mid-point between the two views or directions of perceiving.

Historical sublimes or uncertainties (where two times are felt to coexist, to leak into each other) borrow their shock and excitement from sensory disorientations, disruptions to our sense of scale. Melanie Jackson drew my attention to a phrase used to describe Ruskin's thinking, his tendency 'to botanize and infinitize' with a kind of recklessness about how the different ends of the scale could be brought together. Her works are modest in the means they employ, but often a great distance opens up within them, via suggestion and the play of our imagination with the images and words that pass before us. They are vivid accounts, self-contained but implying something unimagined, the shape of which we have to intuit. The frankness and speed with which the superimposed words set about the business of 'taking you there' is often at odds with the ability of the brain to comprehend *where* it is being led by the images that have been found to accompany those words. Though, unlike dreams, these short works are looped and allow us to revisit the fleeting evidences of the images. Recent works include visits to historically ambiguous places: a Blaenau Ffestiniog slate mine where, during the war, many of the paintings on the walls of the National Gallery hung, and a Brecon village confiscated for military purposes and never returned. Alongside it a model village has been built, for the purposes of military training, complete with blank concrete tombstones in the churchyard, and a house built as a cut-away diagram. (Like any place designed and built at one stroke, it partakes strangely of the ideal, however utilitarian its purpose; though this sense of an ideal, designed place is twinned with the original village, which is both time-arrested at the date of depopulation and also witness to a speeded-up process of ruination. Dramatic evidence of a doubt we may feel applies elsewhere about the ability of time to run everywhere at a uniform pace.) Her works also include imagined journeys to places far removed from the landmass of Britain. These works include footage donated by ciné-camera users, which is then cut together with stories of the kind that keep us transfixed if we find them in a newspaper: of imagined catastrophes, of chance, of meteorite strikes, of ships, of a lighthouse that speaks. The story of the trawler capsized by the collective decision of the herring caught in its nets to dive for the depths is sourced from a reputable Norwegian daily, the *Dagbladet*. Whilst your eye is held by the movement of the ship though the pack-ice that buckles and moves, as the camera slowly pans back, the story – rendered fabulous by its brevity – is sprung on you. It could be encountered in a seventeenth century account and still have the same force of poetry and news. After we are reassured that the six crew members were picked up by another vessel (any disaster needs its survivors, to tell us about it) we can get on with the business of fully enjoying the fearful and wonderful idea of a school of herring that seems to have sensed its fate and to have responded in the only way it could. We insert into the story a moral aspect that fish may exact revenge, and that their action implies a neglected balance between what wealth can be taken from the sea and what the sea may claim in return.

Is the story true? We are not allowed the time to reflect; all the while the words unfold we are eager to hear them. Though the herring is certainly a fish of some mysterious capabilities. After death it glows, and for that reason was taken in baskets by miners in areas of great gas under the earth, so that they could dig out coal by its light, free from the danger of explosions. W G Sebald records in *The Rings of Saturn* that around 1870, when projects for the total illumination of our cities were everywhere afoot, 'two English scientists with the apt names of Herrington and Lightbown investigated the unusual phenomenon in the hope that the luminous substance exuded by dead herrings would lead to a formula for an organic source of light.' And then he writes a sentence that is to me a contemporary manifestation of sublime: 'The failure of this eccentric undertaking, as I read some time ago in a history of artificial light, constituted no more than a negligible setback in the relentless conquest of darkness.' The book is not referenced because Sebald wants us to make a mental journey, to sense the historical space that the phrase 'a history of artificial light' suddenly implies: human history recast as long and mostly dark. As a result of Melanie Jackson's retelling of the capsized herring trawler, the sea is in a similar way sensed again as a vast space that can be descended into, not simply simply sailed over. Our eyes habitually rest on the surface of the sea, avoid thought of how great the depth may be beneath or the dangers that travelling or working on entail. The film footage borrowed to evoke the tale chimes with what we read, but we realise that it cannot be a record of the events. The work is accompanied by a cunningly made miniature trawler, fitted into a bottle, in which it is floated in brine mixed with ink; this recent, dated event has already receded into fabled time, become smaller.

In *0798: New York*, we are in more definitely contemporary seas. The conflict is not between fish and men but between the assumed authority of the US fleet and what turns out to be not another ship but a lighthouse operated by the Canadian coastguards. As an illustration of US military bluster and stupidity, it feels worryingly perfect, almost like an urban myth. The USS Lincoln's mistake makes it appear distinctly ill at ease in what ought to be familiar waters. But the urgency of the rebuke issued by the lighthouse is also, perhaps, distant from the place it appears to speak from. Few of the lighthouses around the world are still inhabited; the machinery is automated and as far as possible controlled remotely. The men who tended the bonfires and lights are replaced by coast-guards surveying their screens; part of the long depopulation of the seas. Perhaps on the island of Sal in Cape Verde there is still a stepped lighthouse fuelled by oil, lit and tended each evening.

* * * * * *

'Ffestiniog: slate here obtained by means of underground adits.' It is sometimes not until an unusual word is encountered that the matter to which it relates and the distance of that matter from us can be more fully understood. In Blaenau Ffestiniog a journey was made to the slate workings at Manod. The entrance to the workings is a dark, rocky opening fringed with ferns. It resembles an idea of a cave from a children's story, but the gate marks it off as property, as a place where mineral rights have been negotiated and are owned and protected. The visitor with her camera follows the guide through the unlocked metal gateway and into the mountain. Inside the gate, the marks left by the railway track in the tunnel lead inwards for a further quarter of a mile. We have no reason to doubt this figure, but we cannot experience the journey in full. The footage is silent but is narrated in captions by the guide, an employee of McAlpine. It is interrupted by frequent, short episodes of blackness in which unknown amounts of time pass. The present tense of description is given to us; and then withheld, a necessary distance.

How to describe a set of underground caverns that are reached by a journey that extends *horizontally* into the side of a mountain? Manod is essentially a slate mine, but the word mine is more often associated with a vertical axis of descent. A journey that continues inwards on the horizontal takes on a mythical aspect through its unfamiliarity. An adit is defined as an approach, a way to go in. At Manod, the way in required some deft phonecalls to McAlpine, Britain's largest housebuilder. But it is refreshing that the rumour that led the way there, and the traditions of secrecy that must have governed the site until 1984, met so little officiousness. The guide, whose Welsh intonation we do not hear but must intuit from his captioned explanations, was keen to share his knowledge on what must have been one of the last permitted trips into the caverns. The State's lease of the caverns for the purposes of safe storage of the paintings from the National Gallery falls into a category of interest that has not for a long time been a secret, but which in the hearing feels it must be. You immediately want to talk about it to someone else: the ghost gallery, the paintings toured to this part of the United Kingdom (for the first time) by a prime minister who until then had been more famous in Wales for bringing in troops to quell rioting coal miners at Tonypandy in 1911. Beyond historical ironies, there is the enduring fantasy of underground spaces.

Reading and journeying differ. One can read about the continuity of historical institutions in the period 1945–89 but in the Manod caverns it can be glimpsed. The maintenance of the brick chambers up until 1984 marks the place as part of the geography of Cold War planning, and brings home the strangeness of that period and the suddenness with which it finally ended. The unplayed European theatre of war involved places like this, not just missiles abstractly pointed as deterrents and tanks massed safely in West Germany, along with any plans for land warfare. The Manod caverns were part of the civil planning in the event of violation of the airspace by those once everyday acronyms, ICBMs. At least two exercises were carried out in the 1970s involving the evacuation of selected pictures from the National Gallery and the Royal Collection. And it turns out that the caverns were maintained on behalf of the Department of Education, not Defence. Some recompense, perhaps, for the century's long export of teachers from Wales, to the benefit of English schools; if the payments had been made on time. Into this century the blue-grey Ordovician slate would have been supplying classrooms as the surface on which children would write, and do their sums …

The captioned visit to Manod is not an act of remystification, it does not pile on the atmospherics. By tracking a tale to its actual, still existent origin the fascination of the story and the place fully emerges and is released from the captivity of half-truths. We do not get all the details that a historian would provide but we don't doubt that they could now be looked up. Any underground spaces generate a disproportionate quantity of rumour, a layering of fiction. They are unusually attractive to the imagination, but there is an alternative: to go there, though not in the greedy way of television. To reinforce this point the video is mute, as if it were a radio broadcast for the eye that stimulates the imagination and the other senses – hearing, touch, sensitivity to temperature. There is no simple, televisual equation of seeing with experiencing. Neither is there any attempt to conceal the fact that travelling involves meeting people and sometimes receiving their help and hospitality. The lack of sound in the works demonstrates one of the purposes of photography: its use as a stimulus to speech, its ability to show tellable events.

* * * * * *

It was sometimes said of slate, during the heyday of the industry, 'it is a stone that does not understand the English'. The history I had expected to encounter when researching the use of the slate mine and the lost village of Epynt was the relationship of Wales to the United Kingdom/England (Churchill's 'island'). I thought I might write about Epynt as Patrick Wright had written about Tyneham in *The Village that Died for England*, Tyneham being the village in a stretch of green Dorset countryside claimed by tank practice and now, like the Mynydd Epynt ranges, tentatively and partially reinventing itself as an environmental and ecological marvel, an 'island' untouched by the century's reliance on agricultural chemicals. But to do that would be to undertake proper history, something I'm not well equipped to do. It seems more appropriate to erect a signpost to *An Uprooted Community: a History of Epynt* by Herbert Hughes (Gomer Press, 1999) for anyone who wants to follow up that story. Melanie Jackson's works are in any case not history, but encounters with places touched by it, with dated events that are marvellous and somehow dateless in their appeal (and, in *0398: Oregon*, with a future tense that is at the same time cancelled by a meteorite and planning to keep its videopoker games going). But her works do involve an imagination for history. It turned out that the title 'soil and seawater' came from Paul Gilroy's important book *The Black Atlantic*. My amateur researches into the history of slate, which follow, had meanwhile led to a linkage between slate and Britain's dominion of the seas.

DNA analysis can now provide answers not just to forensic and medical questions but to ones hitherto classified as archaeological, or hypothetical: the historical origins, migrations and mixing of peoples, knowledge which should hold no fear for anyone. There is no equivalent to DNA analysis for wealth. Money is, in principle, abstract and forgetful of its origins. The landscape of the 1990s is nevertheless haunted by certain calculable but intangible statistics, such as the extent of the military economy. Beyond that, there are certain older patterns of accumulation that originate in periods of history we suppose finished, argued over and done with. Tracing the longevity and continuity of names provides clues to the movements of such money. Another part of the McAlpine slate division, not far from Manod, is Penrhyn quarry. The quarry has been worked for over 400 years, but was notably developed by Richard Pennant, created first Baron Penrhyn of Louth, who revolutionised the slate industry in the 1780s. Leases of slate-rich land were called in, the working arrangements at the quarries were reorganised, transport links were built, such as a horse-drawn tram to the quayside he had constructed at Bangor, and he developed the trade in writing-slates. Other entrepreneurs were stimulated to move into the industry or develop extraction from their lands. The workers themselves profited, and employment through the nineteenth century, though hard, was relatively stable. In 1870, by which time the railway had been built to Portmadoc, which became the main slate port, a quarter of property and profits in Gwynedd could be attributed to slate.

Richard Pennant, Baron Penrhyn, did not just owe his success to slate. The family fortunes derived from sugar plantations in Jamaica and from slaves; the Pennants have been described as 'classic Jamaica nouveaux riches'. As MP for Liverpool, Pennant spoke at Parliament in support of the slave trade. Were the Commons to vote for abolition, Pennant said, 'they actually would strike at seventy millions of property, they ruined the colonies and, by destroying an essential nursery of seamen, gave up dominion of the sea at a single stroke' (Hugh Thomas, *The Slave Trade*, p.513). Pennant died in 1808; the Irish peerage that had been created for him, and which permitted him to enter the lower house as an MP, died with him. But somewhere the commingled profits gained from slate, sugar, slaves and the Penrhyn estate is still in circulation. Quite a lot of it was used by Pennant's great nephew George Dawkins, a later inheritor of Penrhyn quarry, to build Penrhyn Castle, a neo-Norman construction too large to call a folly two miles outside Bangor. It has over 300 rooms and twenty tons of coal a month was required to heat it. The family went on to assemble the largest private collection of paintings in the country, including works by Gainsborough, Canaletto, and Rembrandt; the largest, that is, until the National Gallery came to Manod. Much of the collection can still be found in Penrhyn Castle, along with much intricate slate work. A recent edition of the *Rough Guide to Wales* ranks Pennant's anti-abolitionist stance as the first thing we should know about him. It is not mentioned in the *Dictionary of National Biography*; the *Dictionary of Welsh Biography*, written much later, is more frank. The ebb and flow of historical assumptions can be sensed in these selections of what we need to be told.

I do not know when McAlpine acquired its interests in the slate industry and took over the Penrhyn quarry, but it was from a party held by Alistair McAlpine that Baroness Thatcher emerged to make a comment to the cameras on election night, 1994; a slightly slurred comment I thought. McAlpine has been a prominent Tory. He was given a lifetime peerage – his brother holds the family seat in the Lords – and has been an active peer. He is also a collector, and a book exists about his passion for collecting. When he sold up his collection via auction at Sotheby's, London, it was as though part of the Pitt-Rivers Museum had been unleashed: boxes of neolithic axes, almost worthless as study materials, Anglo-saxon pottery, armour, head-dresses from the south seas, curiosities and some real rarities. The enthusiasm on which the collection was based – and the time it must have taken to assemble – seemed somewhat at odds with the revolutionary forward march of Thatcherism.

The distance from Richard Pennant's slate workings to McAlpine's current operation is considerable. Profits on McAlpine's slate division were down in 1998; just £0·3 million on a turnover of £15·8 million, owing to the strong pound. Assets were valued at £27·2 million and there were only 410 employees. Nevertheless, the Pennant family in the eighteenth and nineteenth centuries and the the McAlpines in the twentieth, demonstrate certain continuities in the proximity of wealth, political patronage and also collecting; an activity artists and amateur historians strongly identify with. And there is still a shock to be encountered by the economic history that can be dug out from any few square miles of these islands. Some historical details still feel like a rumour, like something that should be passed on when encountered, however uncertain we may be about the precise nature of the links between what Paul Gilroy describes as 'modernity's prehistory' and the present.

* * * * * *

'The most important of Burke's rules for the sublime was that the person gaining the terrible delight should not be too close to the object of terror, whatever it was', writes Francis Spufford. It is always thus: the words *large* and *small* are carried about with us in our minds, and we forget real *dimensions*, wrote William Cobbett. Amateur musing about history, as above, is distinguished from professional and proper history by the way it gets historical details, anecdotes and ironies out of proportion with each other; or rather how it does not fully comprehend how hindsight permits some features to emerge at the expense of others that must recede. But most of us are amateurs of history and experience it as something journeyed through, not always feeling sure of what lies on either side. The information received by the eye in particular retains a power to disturb, 'and one's own ocular view and personal conversation will still find out something new and unpointed at by any other'. History is very different when it is printed with pictures.

History is also experienced as a form of time-travel, a delight which can't be left to fiction alone. In Frank Capra's *Lost Horizon* (1937) Shangri-La is discovered by the flight of an aeroplane. It is a curious place; the High Lama, a 200-year-old Belgian Catholic priest, regrets that the mountains all around make radio reception very poor. The film's sentimentality leads inexorably to a conclusion that though we may not all get to this particular happy valley, it probably lurks in our own breast. But the appeal of a journey through space that turns out to be a journey in time is not eliminated by this ending: it dramatises our suspicion that time does not move everywhere at the same rate, that disturbances to our sense of time have a power to reveal something about the vantage point from which we habitually do our surveying. After watching *Lost Horizon* and Melanie Jackson's silent visual works with words, I dreamed about contemporary radio reports from a troubled West African state; radio reports, but with pictures somehow attached. I cannot explain that part. The words of the report were so clear that I could picture the events described, and these pictures seemed to be broadcast directly to a receiver in my brain, but they were not television pictures. With the advantage of hindsight I rationalise the dream into a wish that there is a place where somehow the intelligence received by the ear and by the eye will be reconciled. In the meantime artistic investigation is available that anticipates this mental technology, and allows us to hear eyewitness and to watch hearsay, to go voyaging.

The Three Rivers Programme devised by Cardiff Bay Arts Trust provided opportunities for artists to explore the nature and environs of the three main rivers Taff, Ely and Rhymney, flowing through Cardiff into the Bristol Channel.

Melanie Jackson held the River Rhymney fellowship throughout 1998 working to develop the remarkable city-wide *llath*yard project, culminating in **soil & seawater.**

The programme was initiated by Cardiff Bay Arts Trust in collaboration with the University of Wales Institute Cardiff with financial assistance from Cardiff Bay Development Corporation and the Foundation for Sports and the Arts.

This book is dedicated to Brian Williams, Marcus Bischoff and Joyce Kent

The artist wishes to thank Carole-Anne Davies, Nigel Hughes, Robin Klassnik, Wiard Sterk, Zedekiah

Designed by Phil Baines
Printed & bound by
B·A·S Printers Limited

Matt's Gallery is funded by the London Arts Board

Foundation for sport and the arts

CARDIFF BAY

Cardiff Bay Arts Trust

LONDON ARTS BOARD

UWIC Centre for Research in Fine Art

ELECTROHOME